GREAT
CAPTAINS

GREAT CAPTAINS

THE ART OF WAR IN THE
CAMPAIGNS OF ALEXANDER,
HANNIBAL, CAESAR,
GUSTAVUS ADOLPHUS,
FREDERICK THE GREAT,
AND NAPOLEON

THEODORE A. DODGE

BARNES
&NOBLE
BOOKS
NEW YORK

Originally published in 1889.

This edition published by Barnes & Noble, Inc.

1995 Barnes & Noble Books

ISBN 1-56619-855-0

Printed and bound in the United States of America

M 9 8 7 6 5 4 3 2 1

CONTENTS.

LIST OF MAPS.

LECTURE I.

ALEXANDER.

THE earliest history is but a record of wars. Peace had no events stirring enough to call for record. It was the conflict of heroes which inspired the oldest and still greatest of poems. As the more intelligent peoples were, as a rule, the victors, the march of civilization followed in the footsteps of war up to very recent times. The history of war has been carefully recorded for nearly twenty-five centuries, but the science of war, in a written form, dates back less than one hundred years.

The art of war owes its origin and growth to the deeds of a few great captains. Not to their brilliant victories; not to the noble courage evoked by their ambition; not to their distortion of mechanics and the sciences into new engines of slaughter; not to their far-reaching conquests; but to their intellectual conceptions. For war is as highly intellectual as astronomy. The main distinction between the one and the other lies in the fact that the intellectual conception of the general must at once be so put into play as to call for the exertion of the moral forces of his character, while the astronomer's inspiration stops at a purely mental process. What has produced the great captains is the coexistence of extraordinary intellect and equal force of character, coupled with events worthy of and calling out these qualities in their highest expression.

My effort will be to suggest how, out of the campaigns and battles of the great captains, has arisen what to-day we call the art of war, — not so much out of the technical details, which are a subordinate matter, as the general scheme; and to show that, while war is governed by its rules as well as art, it is the equipment of the individual which makes an Alexander or a Michael Angelo. Six of these captains stand distinctly in a class by themselves, far above any others. They are, in ancient days, Alexander, Hannibal, Cæsar, — all within three hundred years of each other. Then follows a gap of seventeen centuries of unmethodical war, and we complete the list with Gustavus Adolphus, Frederick, and Napoleon, — all within two centuries. "The art of war is the most difficult of all arts, the military reputation in general the greatest of all reputations," says Napoleon. The limited number of great captains proves this true.

The words *campaign* and *battle* cover the same ground as *strategy* and *tactics*. Let me make these plain to you, and I shall have done with definitions and technicalities. A campaign consists in the marching of an army about the country or into foreign territory to seek the enemy or inflict damage on him. Strategy is the complement of this term, and is the art of so moving an army over a country, — on the map, as it were, — that when you meet the enemy you shall have placed him in a disadvantageous position for battle or other manœuvres. One or more battles may occur in a campaign. Tactics (or grand tactics, to distinguish the art from the mere details of drill) relates only to and is coextensive with the evolutions of the battle-field. Strategy comprehends your manœuvres when not in the presence of the enemy ; tactics, your manœuvres when in contact with him. Tactics has always existed as common military knowledge, often in much perfection. Strategy is of modern creation, *as an art which one may study.* But all great captains have been great strategists.

To say that strategy is war on the map is no figure of speech. Napoleon always planned and conducted his campaigns on maps of the country spread out for him by his staff, and into these maps he stuck colored pins to indicate where his divisions were to move. Having thus wrought out his plan, he issued orders accordingly. To the general, the map is a chessboard, and upon this he moves his troops as you or I move queen and knight.

Previous to Cyrus, about 550 B.C., we have a record of nothing

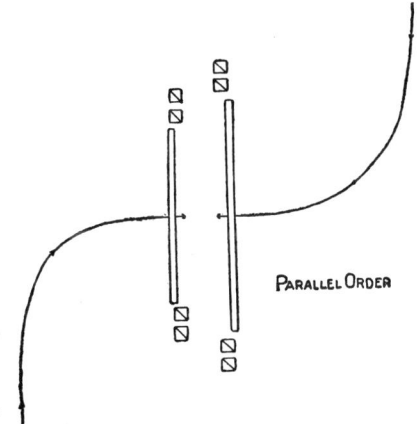

PARALLEL ORDER

useful to the modern soldier. Nimrod, Semiramis, Sesostris were no doubt distinguished conquerors. But they have left nothing for us to profit by. War was a physical, not an intellectual art, for many centuries. Armies marched out to meet each other, and, if an ambush was not practicable, drew up in parallel order, and fought till one gave way. The greater force could form the longer line and overlap and turn the other's flanks. And then, as to-day, a flank attack was fatal; for men cannot fight unless they face the foe ; and a line miles in length needs time to change its front.

Cyrus is to the soldier the first historical verity. In the battle of Thymbra, according to Xenophon, where

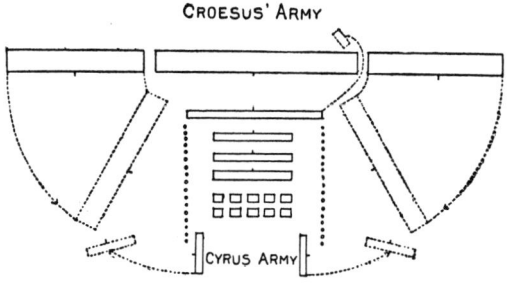

BATTLE OF THYMBRA B C. 545

Crœsus outnumbered him more than two to one and overlapped his flanks, he disposed his troops in so deep a tactical order of five lines, and so well protected his flanks, that when Crœsus' wings wheeled in to encompass him, his reserves in the fifth line could fall on the flanks of these very wheeling wings. And as the wheel was extensive and difficult of execution, it produced a gap between wing and centre, — as Cyrus had expected, —

and into this he poured with a chosen body, took Crœsus' centre in reverse, and utterly overthrew him and his kingdom. Cyrus overran in his conquests almost as great a territory as Alexander.

It is of advantage to see what had been done before Alexander's time, — to understand how much Alexander knew of war from others. For Alexander found war in a crude state and conducted it with the very highest art. That his successors did not do so is due to the fact that they did not understand, or were not capable of imitating him.

Cyrus' successor, Darius I. (B.C. 513), undertook a campaign against the Scythians north of the Danube, with, it is said, seven hundred thousand men. The Greek Mandrocles bridged for this army both the Bosphorus and the Danube, no mean engineering feat to-day.

Shortly after came the Persian invasion of Greece and the battle of Marathon (490 B.C.). Here occurred one of the early tactical variations from the parallel order. Miltiades had but eleven thousand men ; the Persians had ten times as many. They lay on the sea-shore in front of their fleet. To reach and lean his flanks on two brooks running to the sea, Miltiades made his centre thin, his wings strong, and advanced sharply on the enemy. As was inevitable, the deep Persian line easily broke through his centre. But Miltiades had either anticipated and prepared his army for this, or else seized the occasion by a very stroke of genius. There was no symptom of demoralization. The Persian troops followed hard after the defeated centre. Miltiades caused each wing to wheel inwards, and fell upon both flanks of the Persian advance, absolutely overwhelming it, and throwing it back upon the main line in such confusion as to lead to complete victory.

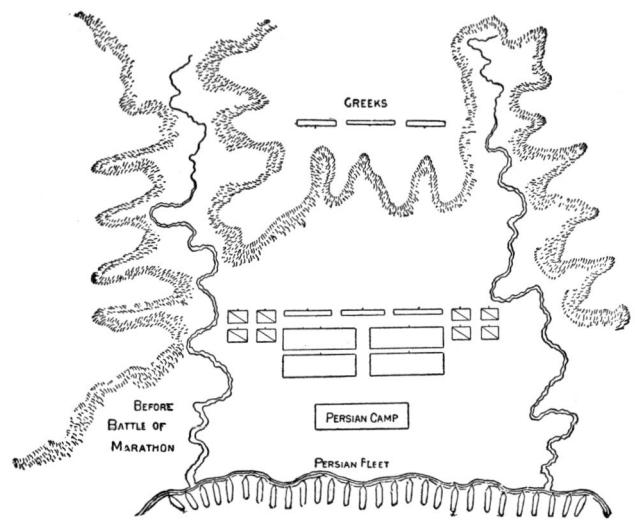

You must note that demoralization always plays an immense part in battle. The Old Dessauer capped all battle-tactics with his : " Wenn Du gehst nicht zurück, so geht der Feind zurück ! " (If you don't fall back, why, the enemy will fall back.) Whenever a tactical manœuvre unnerves the enemy, it at once transforms his army into a mob. The reason why Pickett's charge did not succeed was that there was no element of demoralization in the Union ranks. Had there been, Gettysburg might have become a rebel victory.

The Peloponnesian War shows instances of far-seeing strategy, such as the seizure of Pylos (B.C. 425), whence the threat of incursions on Sparta's rear obliged her to relax her hold on the throat of Athens. Brasidas was the general who, at this time, came nearest to showing the moral and intellectual combination of the great soldier. His marches through Thessaly and Illyria and his defeat of Cleon at Amphipolis were admirable. He it was who

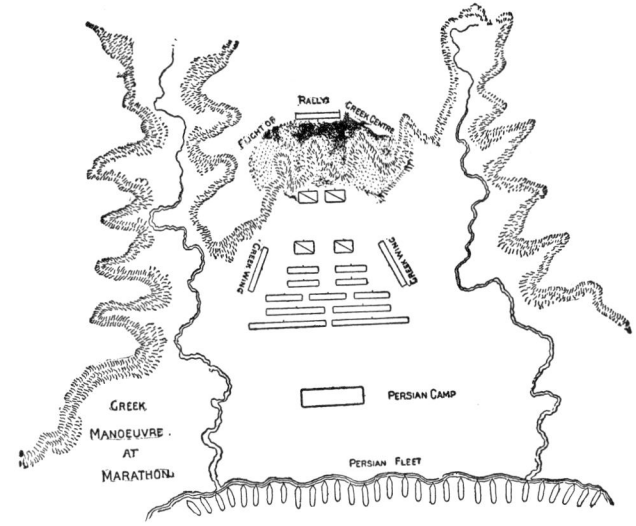

first marched in a hollow square, with baggage in the centre.

The soldier of greatest use to us preceding Alexander was unquestionably Xenophon. After participating in the defeat of Cyrus the Younger by Artaxerxes, at Cunaxa (B.C. 401), in which battle the Greek phalanx had held its own against twenty times its force, Xenophon was chosen to command the rear-guard of the phalanx in the Retreat of the Ten Thousand to the Sea;

and it is he who has shown the world what should be the tactics of retreat, — how to command a rear-guard. No chieftain ever possessed a grander moral ascendant over his men. More tactical originality has come from the Anabasis than from any dozen other books. For instance, Xenophon describes accurately a charge over bad ground in which, so to speak, he broke forward by the right of companies, — one of the most useful minor manœuvres. He built a bridge on goat-skins stuffed with hay, and sewed up so as to be water-tight. He established a reserve in rear of the phalanx from which to feed weak parts of the line, — a superb first conception. He systematically devastated the country traversed to arrest pursuit. After the lapse of twenty-three centuries there is no better military text-book than the Anabasis.

Alexander had a predecessor in the invasion of Asia. Agesilaus, King of Sparta, went (B.C. 399) to the assistance of the Greek cities of Asia Minor, unjustly oppressed by Tissaphernes. He set sail with eight thousand men and landed at Ephesus; adjusted the difficulties of these cities, and, having conducted two successful campaigns in Phrygia and Caria, returned to Lacedemon overland.

Associated with one of the most notable tactical manœuvres — the oblique order of battle — is the immortal name of Epaminondas. This great soldier originated what all skilful generals have used frequently and to effect, and what Frederick the Great showed in its highest perfection at Leuthen. As already observed, armies up to that time had with rare exceptions attacked in parallel order and fought until one or other gave way. At Leuctra (B.C. 371), Epaminondas had six thousand men, against eleven thousand of the invincible Spartans.

The Thebans were dispirited by many failures, the Lacedemonians in good heart. The Spartan king was on the right of his army. Epaminondas tried a daring innovation.

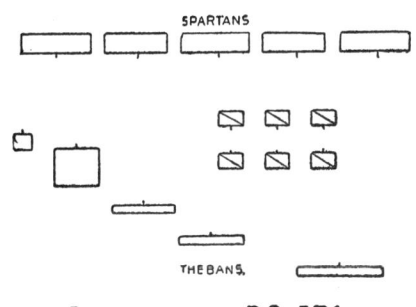

BATTLE OF LEUCTRA B.C. 371

He saw that if he could break the Spartan right, he would probably drive the enemy from the field. He therefore quadrupled the depth of his own left, making it a heavy column, led it sharply forward, and ordered his centre and right to advance more slowly, so as not seriously to engage. The effect was never doubtful. While the Spartan centre and left was held in place by the threatening attack of the Theban centre and right, as well as the combat of the cavalry between the lines, their right was overpowered and crushed; having defeated which, Epaminondas wheeled around on the flank of the Spartan centre and left, and swept them from the field. The genius of a great tactician had prevailed over numbers, prestige, and confidence. At Mantinœa, nine years later, Epaminondas practised the same manœuvre with equal success, but himself fell in the hour of victory. (B.C. 362.)

The Greek phalanx was the acme of shock tactics. It was a compact body, sixteen men deep, whose long spears bristled to the front in an array which for defence or attack on level ground made it irresistible. No body of troops could withstand its impact. Only on broken ground was it weak. Iphicrates, of Athens, had developed the capacity of light troops by a well-planned skirmish-drill and discipline, and numbers of these accompanied each phalanx, to protect its flanks and curtain its advance.

Such, then, had been the progress in military art when Alexander the Great was born. Like Hannibal and Frederick, Alexander owed his military training and his army to his father. Philip had been a hostage in Thebes in his youth, had studied the tactics of Epaminondas, and profited by his lessons. When he ascended the throne of Macedon, the army was but a rabble. He made and left it the most perfect machine of ancient days. He armed his phalanx with the sarissa, a pike twenty-one feet long, and held six feet from the loaded butt. The sarissas of the five front ranks protruded from three to fifteen feet beyond the line; and all were interlocked. This formed a wall of spears which nothing could penetrate. The Macedonian phalanx was perfectly drilled in a fashion much like our evolutions in column, and was distinctly the best in Greece. It was unconquered till later opposed by the greater mobility of the Roman legion. The cavalry was equally well drilled. Before Philip's death, in all departments, from the ministry of war down, the army of Macedon was as perfect in all its details as the army of Prussia is to-day.

Philip also made, and Alexander greatly improved, what was the equivalent of modern artillery. The catapult was a species of huge bow, capable of throwing pikes weighing from ten to three hundred pounds over half a mile. It could also hurl a large number of leaden bullets at each fire. It was the cannon of the ancients. The ballista was their mortar, and threw heavy stones with accurate aim to a considerable distance. It could cast flights of arrows. Alexander constructed and was always accompanied by batteries of ballistas and catapults, the essential parts of which were even more readily transported than our mountain batteries. These were not, however, commonly used in battle, but rather in the attack and defence of defiles, positions, and towns.

Alexander's first experience in a pitched battle was at Chœronea (B.C. 338), on which field Philip won his election as Autocrator, or general-in-chief, of the armies of Greece. Here, a lad of eighteen, Alexander commanded the Macedonian left wing, and defeated the hitherto invincible Theban Sacred Band by his repeated and obstinate charges at the head of the Thessalian horse. Philip had for years harbored designs of an expedition against the Persian monarchy, but did not live to carry them out. Alexander succeeded him at the age of twenty (B.C. 336). He had been educated under Aristotle. No monarch of his years was ever so well equipped as he in head and heart. Like Frederick, he was master from the start. "Though the name has changed, the king remains," quoth he. His arms he found ready to hand, tempered in his father's forge. But it was his own strength and skill which wielded them.

The Greeks considered themselves absolved from Macedonian jurisdiction by the death of Philip. Not so thought Alexander. He marched against them, turning the passes of Tempe and Kallipeuke by hewing a path along the slopes of Mount Ossa, and made himself master of Thessaly. The Amphictyonic Council deemed it wise to submit, and elected him Autocrator in place of his father.

Alexander's one ambition had always been to head the Greeks in punishing the hereditary enemy of Hellas, the Persian king. He had imbibed the idea of his Asiatic conquests in his early youth, and had once, as a lad, astonished the Persian envoys to the Court of Pella by his searching and intelligent questions concerning the peoples and resources of the East.

Before starting on such an expedition, however, he must once for all settle the danger of barbarian incursions along his borders. This he did in a campaign brilliant by its skilful audacity; but on a rumor of his defeat and death among the savages, Thebes again revolted. Alexander, by a march of three hundred miles in two weeks across a mountainous country, suddenly appeared at her gates, captured and destroyed the city, and sold the inhabitants into slavery. Athens begged off. Undisputed chief, he now set out for Asia with thirty thousand foot and five thousand horse. (B.C. 334.)

There is time but for the description of a single campaign and battle of this great king's. The rest of his all but superhuman exploits must be hurried through with barely a mention, and the tracing of his march on the map. I have preferred to select for longer treatment the battle of the Hydaspes, for Issus and Arbela are more generally familiar.

Alexander's first battle after crossing into Asia was at the Granicus, where he defeated the Persian army with the loss of a vast number of their princes and generals. Thence he advanced through Mysia and Lydia, freeing the Greek cities on the way, captured Miletus and Halicarnassus, and having made himself a necessary base on the Ægean, marched through Caria and Lycia, fighting for every step, but always victorious, not merely by hard blows, but by hard blows delivered where they would best tell. Then through Phrygia to Gordium (where he cut the Gordian knot), and through Cappadocia to Cilicia. He then passed through the Syrian Gates — a mountain gap — heading for Phœnicia. Here Darius got in his rear by passing through the Amanic Gates farther up the range, which Alexander either did not know, or singularly enough had overlooked. The Macedonians were absolutely cut off from their communications. But, nothing daunted, Alexander kept his men in heart, turned on Darius, and defeated him at Issus, with a skill only equalled by his hopeful boldness, and saved himself harmless from the results of a glaring error.

So far (B.C. 333), excepting this, Alexander had taken no step which left any danger in his rear. He had confided every city and country he had traversed to the hands of friends. His advance was our first instance on a grand scale of methodical war, — the origin of strategy. He continued in this course, not proposing to risk himself in the heart of Persia until he had reduced to control the entire coast-line of the Eastern Mediterranean as a base. This task led him through Syria, Phœnicia, — where the siege of Tyre, one of the few greatest sieges of antiquity, delayed him seven months, — and Palestine to Egypt. Every part of this enormous stretch of coast was subjugated.

Having in possession, practically, all the seaports of the then civilized world, and having neutralized the Persian fleet by victories on land and at sea, Alexander returned to Syria, marched inland and crossed the Euphrates and Tigris, thus projecting his line of advance from the centre of his base. At Arbela he defeated the Persian army in toto, though they were twenty to his one. Babylon, Susa, Persepolis, and Pasargadæ opened their gates to the conqueror. But Darius escaped.

It was now the spring of 330 B.C. Only four years had elapsed and Alexander had overturned the Persian Empire ; and though he left home with a debt of eight hundred talents, he had won a treasure estimated at from one hundred and fifty millions of dollars up.

Alexander now followed Darius through Media and the Caspian Gates to Parthia, subduing the several territories he traversed. He found Darius murdered by the satraps who attended him. This was no common disappointment to Alexander, for the possession of the person of the Great King would have not only rendered his further conquests more easy, but would have ministered enormously to his

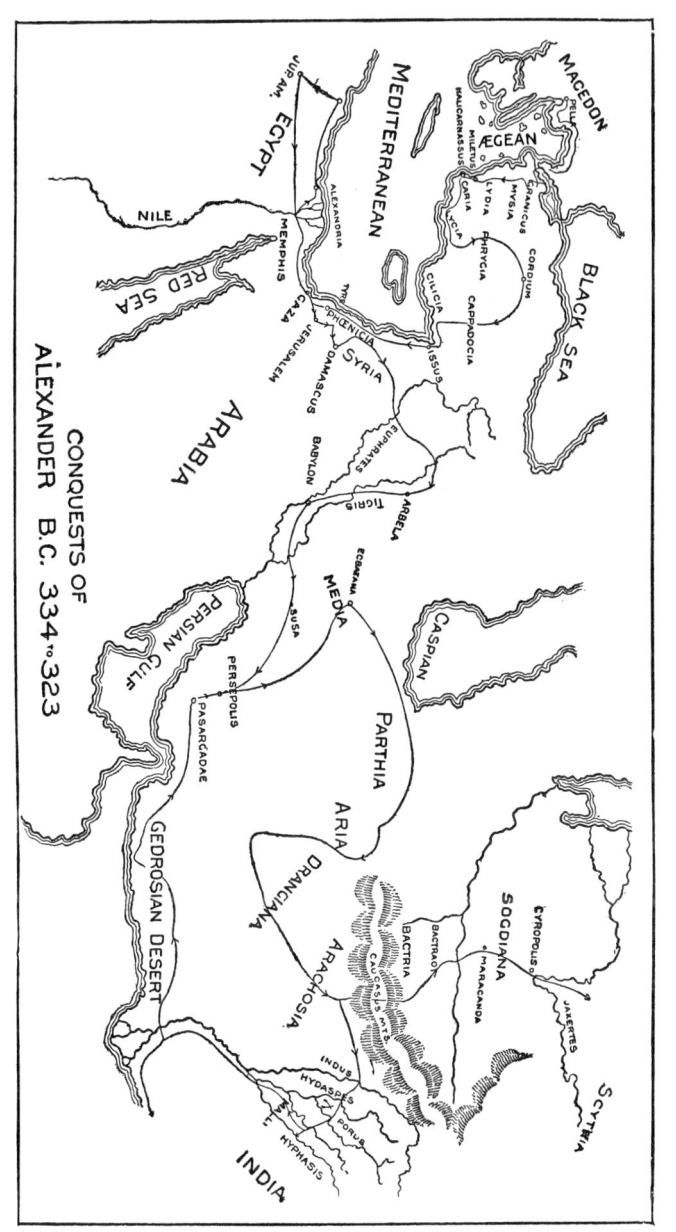

CONQUESTS OF
ALEXANDER B.C. 334 to 323

natural and fast-growing vanity. He pursued the murderers of Darius, but as he could not safely leave enemies in his rear, he was compelled to pause and reduce Aria, Drangiana, and Arachosia. Then he made his way over the Caucasus into Bactria and Sogdiana, the only feat which equals Hannibal's passage of the Alps. His eastern limit was the river Jaxertes, the crossing of which was made under cover of his artillery, — its first use for such a purpose. The details of all these movements are so wonderful and show such extraordinary courage, enterprise, and intelligence, such exceptional power over men, so true a conception of the difficulties to be encountered, such correct judgment as to the best means of overcoming them, that if the test should be the accomplishment of the all but impossible, Alexander would easily stand at the head of all men who have ever lived. He now formed the project of conquering India, and, returning over the Caucasus, marched to the Indus and crossed it. Other four years had been consumed since he left Persepolis. It was May, B.C. 326.

Alexander was in the Punjaub, the land of the five rivers. The Hydaspes was swollen with the storms of the rainy season and the melting snows of the Himalayas. The roads were execrable. On the farther side of the river, a half-mile wide, could be seen Porus, noted as the bravest and most able king in India, with his army drawn up before his camp and his elephants and war-chariots in front, ready to dispute his crossing. The Hydaspes is nowhere fordable, except in the dry season. Alexander saw that he could not force a passage in the face of this

array, and concluded to manœuvre for a chance to cross.
He had learned from experience that the Indians were
good fighters. His cavalry could not be made to face
their elephants. He was reduced to stratagem, and what
he did has ever since been the model for the passage of
rivers, when the enemy occupies the other bank. Alexander first tried to convince Porus that he intended to

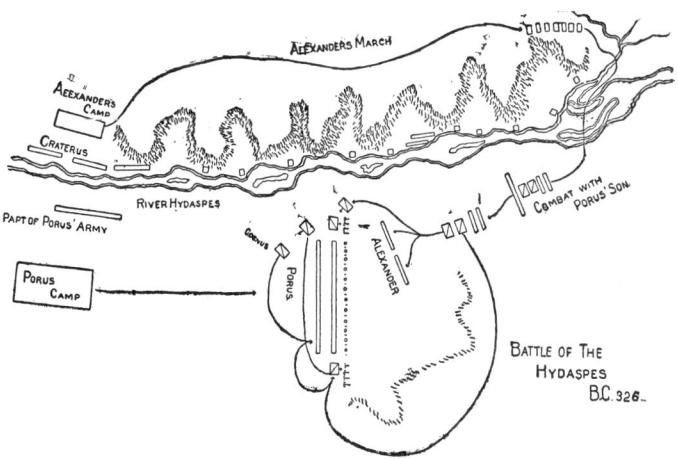

wait till the river fell, and carefully spread a rumor to
this effect. He devastated the country, accumulated vast
stores in his camp, and settled his troops in quarters.
Porus continued active in scouting the river-banks, and
held all the crossings in force. Alexander sent parties in
boats up and down the stream to distract his attention.
He made many feints at crossing by night. He put the
phalanx under arms in the light of the camp-fires; blew
the signals to move; marched the horse up and down; got
the boats ready to load. To oppose all this Porus would

bring down his elephants to the banks, order his men under arms, and so remain till daylight, lest he should be surprised.

After some time Porus began to weary his troops by marching them out in the inclement weather to forestall attempts to cross ; and finding these never actually made, grew careless, believing that Alexander would, in reality, make no serious effort till low water. But Alexander was daily watching his opportunity. He saw that to cross in front of Porus' camp was still impossible. The presence of the elephants near the shore would surely prevent the horse from landing, and even his infantry was somewhat unnerved by them. But he had learned that large reën-forcements were near at hand for Porus, and it was essential to defeat the Indians before these came to hand.

The right bank, on which lay the Macedonians, was high and hilly. The left bank was a wide, fertile plain. Alexander could hide his movements, while observing those of Porus. When he saw that the Indian king had ceased to march out to meet his feigned crossings, he began to prepare for a real one, meanwhile keeping up the blind. Seventeen miles above the camp was a wooded headland formed by a bend in the river and a small afflu-ent, capable of concealing a large force, and itself hidden by a wooded and uninhabited island in its front. This place Alexander connected by a chain of couriers with the camp, and laid posts all along the river, at which, every night, noisy demonstrations were made and numerous fires were lighted, as if large forces were present at each of them. When Porus had been quite mystified as to

Alexander's intentions, Craterus was left with a large part of the army at the main camp, and instructed to make open preparations to cross, but not really to do so unless Porus' army and the elephants should move up-stream. Between Craterus and the headland, Alexander secreted another large body, with orders to put over when he should have engaged battle. He himself marched, well back of the river and out of sight, — there was no dust to betray him, — to the headland, where preparations had already been completed for crossing.

The night was tempestuous. The thunder and rain, usual during the south-west monsoon, drowned the noise of the workmen and moving troops and concealed the camp-fires, as well as kept Porus' outposts under shelter. Alexander had caused a number of boats to be cut in two for transportation, but in such manner that they could be quickly joined for use, — the first mention we have of anything like pontoons. Towards daylight the storm abated and the crossing began. Most of the infantry and the heavy cavalry were put over in the boats. The light cavalry swam across, each man sustaining himself on a hay-stuffed skin, so as not to burden the horses. The movement was not discovered until the Macedonians had passed the island, when Porus' scouts saw what was doing and galloped off with the news. It soon appeared that the army had not landed on the mainland, but on a second island. This was usually accessible by easy fords, but the late rains had swollen the low water from it to the shore to ɐ deep and rapid torrent. Here was a dilemma. Unless the troops were at once got over, Porus would be down upon them. There was no time to bring the boats around the island. After some delay and a great many accidents, a place was found where, by wading to their breasts, the infantry could get across. This was done, and the cavalry, already over, was thrown out in front. Alexander, as speedily as possible, set out with his horse, some five thousand strong, and ordered the phalanx, which numbered about six thousand more, to follow on in column, the light foot to keep up, if possible, with the cavalry. He was afraid that Porus might retire, and wished to be on hand to pursue.

Porus could see the bulk of the army under Craterus still occupying the old camp, and knew that the force which had crossed could be but a small part of the army. But he underestimated it, and instead of moving on it in force, sent only some two thousand cavalry and one hundred and twenty chariots, under his son, to oppose it. Porus desired to put off battle till his reënforcements came up. Alexander proposed to force battle.

So soon as Alexander saw that he had but a limited force in his front, he charged down upon it with the heavy horse, " squadron by squadron," says Arrian, which must have meant something similar to our line in *echelon*, while the light horse skirmished about its flanks. The enemy was at once broken, and Porus' son and four hundred men were killed. The chariots, stalled in the deep bottom, were one and all captured.

Porus was nonplussed. Alexander's manœuvre had been intended to deceive, and had completely deceived him. He could see Craterus preparing to cross, and yet he knew

Alexander to be the more dangerous of the two. He was uncertain what to do, but finally concluded to march against Alexander, leaving some elephants and an adequate force opposite Craterus. He had with him four thousand cavalry, three hundred chariots, two hundred elephants, and thirty thousand infantry. Having moved some distance, he drew up his lines on a plain where the ground was solid, and awaited Alexander's attack.

His arrangements were skilful. In front were the redoubtable elephants, which Porus well knew that Alexander's cavalry could not face, one hundred feet apart, covering the entire infantry line, some four miles long. The infantry had orders to fill up the gaps between the elephants by companies of one hundred and fifty men. Columns of foot flanked the elephants. These creatures were intended to keep the Macedonian horse at a distance, and trample down the foot when it should advance on the Indian lines. Porus had but the idea of a parallel order, and of a defensive battle at that. His own cavalry was on the wings, and in their front the chariots, each containing two mailed drivers, two heavy and two light-armed men.

When the Macedonian squadrons reached the ground, and the king rode out to reconnoitre, he saw that he must wait for his infantry, and began manœuvring with his horse, to hold himself till the phalanx came up. Had Porus at once advanced on him, he could easily have swept him away. But that he did not do so was of a part with Alexander's uniform good fortune. The phalanx came up at a lively gait, and the king gave it a breathing-spell, while he kept Porus busy by small

demonstrations. The latter, with his elephants, and three
to one of men, simply bided his time, calmly confident of
the result. Alexander yielded honest admiration to the
skill of Porus' dispositions, and his forethought in oppos-
ing the elephants to his own strong arm, the cavalry.

The Macedonians had advanced with their right leaning
on the river. Despite the elephants, Alexander must use
his horse, if he expected to win. In this arm he outnumbered the enemy. He could not attack in front, nor, indeed, await the onset of the elephants and chariots. With
the instinct of genius, and confident that his army could
manœuvre with thrice the rapidity of Porus, as well as
himself think and act still more quickly, he determined to
attack the Indian left in force. He despatched Coenus
with a body of heavy horse by a circuit against the
enemy's right, with instructions, if Porus' cavalry of that
wing should be sent to the assistance of the left, to charge
in on the naked flank and rear of the Indian infantry. He
himself with the bulk and flower of the horse, sustained
by the more slowly moving phalanx, made an oblique
movement towards Porus' left. The Indian king at first
supposed that Alexander was merely uncovering his infantry, to permit it to advance to the attack, and as such
an attack would be playing into Porus' hands, he awaited
results. This, again, was Alexander's salvation. It left
him the offensive. Porus had not yet perceived Coenus'
march, the probably rolling ground had hidden it, and he
ordered his right-flank cavalry over to sustain that of the
left, towards which flank Alexander was moving. The
phalanx, once uncovered, Alexander ordered forward, but

not to engage until the wings had been attacked, so as to neutralize the elephants and the chariots.

These dispositions gave the Macedonian line the oblique order of Epaminondas, with left refused. Alexander had used the same order at Issus and Arbela. As he rode forward, he pushed out the Daan horse-bowmen to skirmish with the Indian left, while he, in their rear, by a half wheel, could gain ground to the right sufficient to get beyond and about the enemy's flank, with the heavy squadrons of Hephæstion and Perdiccas. The Indian horse seems to have been misled by what Alexander was doing, — it probably could not understand the Macedonian tactics, — for it was not well in hand, and had advanced out of supporting distance from the infantry.

Meanwhile Coenus had made his circuit of the enemy's right, and, the Indian cavalry having already moved over towards the left, he fell on the right flank and rear of the Indian infantry and threw it into such confusion that it was kept inactive during the entire battle. Then, completing his gallant ride, and with the true instinct of the *beau sabreur*, Coenus galloped along Porus' rear, to join the *mêlée* already engaged on the left. To oppose Coenus as well as Alexander, the Indian cavalry was forced to make double front. While effecting this, Alexander drove his stoutest charge home upon them. They at once broke and retired upon the elephants, "as to a friendly wall for refuge," says Arrian.

A number of these beasts were now made to wheel to the left and charge on Alexander's horse, but this exposed them in flank to the phalanx, which advanced, wounded many of the animals, and killed most of the drivers. Deprived of guidance, the elephants swerved on the phalangites, but they were received with such a shower of darts that in their affright they made about-face upon the Indian infantry, to the great consternation of the latter.

The Indian cavalry, meanwhile, had rallied under the cover of the elephants, and again faced the Macedonians. But the king renewed his charges again and again, — it was a characteristic feat of Alexander's, from boyhood up, to be able to get numberless successive charges out of his squadrons, — and forced them back under the brutes' heels. The Macedonian cavalry was itself much disorganized; but Alexander's white plume waved everywhere, and under his inspiration, Coenus having now joined, there was, despite disorder, no let-up to the pressure, from both fronts at once, on Porus' harassed horse.

The situation was curious. The Macedonian cavalry, inspired by the tremendous animation of the king, maintained its constant charges. The Indian cavalry was huddled up close to the infantry and elephants. These unwieldy creatures were alternately urged on the phalanx and driven back on Porus' line. The Macedonian infantry had plenty of elbow-room, and could retire from them and again advance. The Indian infantry had none. But finally the elephants grew discouraged at being between two fires, lifted their trunks with one accord in a trumpeting of terror, and retired out of action, "like ships backing water," as Arrian picturesquely describes it.

Alexander now saw that the victory was his. But the situation was still delicate; he kept the phalanx in place and continued his charges upon Porus' left flank with the cavalry. Finally, Porus, who had been in the thickest of the fray, collected forty of the yet unwounded elephants, and charged on the phalanx, leading the van with his own huge, black, war-elephant. But Alexander met this desperate charge with the Macedonian archers, who swarmed around the monsters, wounded some, cut the ham-strings of others, and killed the drivers.

The charge had failed. At this juncture, — his eye was as keen as Napoleon's for the critical instant, — Alexander ordered forward the phalanx, with protended sarissas and linked shields, while himself led the cavalry round to the Indian rear, and charged in one final effort with the terrible Macedonian shout of victory. The whole Indian army was reduced to an inert, paralyzed mass. It was only individuals who managed to escape.

The battle had lasted eight hours, and had been won against great odds by crisp tactical skill and the most brilliant use of cavalry. The history of war shows no instance of a more superb and effective use of horse. Coenus exhibited, in carrying out the king's orders, the clean-cut conception of the cavalry general's duty, and Alexander's dispositions were masterly throughout. His prudent forethought in leaving behind him a force sufficient to insure his safety in case of disaster in the battle is especially to be noted.

Craterus and the other detachments now came up, and the pursuit was intrusted to them. Of Porus' army, twenty thousand infantry and three thousand cavalry, including numberless chiefs, were killed, and all the chariots, which had proved useless in the battle, were broken up. The Macedonian killed numbered two hundred horse and seven hundred foot. The wounded were not usually counted, but averaged eight to twelve for one of killed. This left few Macedonians who could not boast a wound.

Porus, himself wounded, endeavored to escape on his own elephant. Alexander galloped after on Bucephalus, the horse we all remember that, as a mere lad, he had mounted and controlled by kindness and by skilful, rational treatment, when all others had failed to do so, and who had served him ever since. But the gallant old charger, exhausted by the toils of the day, fell in his tracks and died, at the age of upwards of thirty years. Porus surrendered, when he might have escaped. When brought to Alexander, the king, in admiration of his bravery and skill, asked him what treatment he would like to receive. " That due to a king, Alexander ! " proudly replied Porus. " Ask thou more of me," said Alexander. " To be treated like a king covers all a king can desire," insisted the Indian monarch. Alexander, recognizing the qualities of the man, made Porus his friend, associate, and ally, and viceroy of a large part of his Punjaub conquests.

The Macedonian king went but a short distance farther into India. His project of reaching the Ganges was shipwrecked on the determination of his veterans not to advance beyond the Hyphasis. He returned to the Hydaspes, and moved down the river on a huge fleet of two thousand boats, subduing the tribes on either bank as he proceeded on his way. In capturing a city of the Malli he nearly met his death.

This episode is too characteristic of the man to pass by unnoticed. Battles were won in those days by hand-to-hand work, and Alexander always fought like a Homeric hero. He had formed two storming columns, himself heading the one and Perdiccas the other. The Indians but weakly defended the town wall, and retired into the citadel. Alexander at once made his way into the town through a gate which he forced, but Perdiccas was delayed for want of scaling-ladders. Arrived at the citadel, the Macedonians began to undermine its wall, and the ladders were put in position. Alexander, always impatient in his valor, seeing that the work did not progress as fast as his own desires, seized a scaling-ladder, himself planted it, and ascended first of all, bearing his shield aloft, to ward off the darts from above. He was followed by Peucestas, the soldier who always carried before the king in battle the shield brought from the temple of the Trojan Athena, and by Leonnatus, the confidential body-guard. Upon an adjoining ladder went Abreas, a soldier who received double pay for his conspicuous valor. Alexander first mounted the battlements and frayed a place for himself with his sword. The king's guards, anxious for his safety, crowded upon the ladders in such numbers as to break them down. Alexander was left standing with only Peucestas, Abreas, and Leonnatus upon the wall in the midst of his enemies; but so indomitable were his strength and daring that none came within reach of his sword but to fall. The barbarians had recognized him by his armor and white plume, and the multitude of darts which fell upon him threatened his life at every instant. The Macedonians below implored him to leap down into their outstretched arms. Nothing daunted, however, and calling on every man to follow who loved him, Alexander leaped down inside the wall and, with his three companions backing up against it, stoutly held his own. In a brief moment he had cut down a number of Indians and had slain their leader, who ventured against him. But Abreas fell dead beside him, with an arrow in the forehead, and Alexander was at the same moment pierced by an arrow through the breast. The king valiantly stood his ground till he fell exhausted by loss of blood, and over him, like lions at bay, but glowing with heroic lustre, stood Peucestas, warding missiles from him with the sacred shield, and Leonnatus guarding him with his sword, both dripping blood from many wounds. It seemed that the doom of all was sealed.

The Macedonians, meanwhile, some with ladders and some by means of pegs inserted between the stones in the wall, had begun to reach the top, and one by one leaped within and surrounded the now lifeless body of Alexander. Others forced an entrance through one of the gates and flew to the rescue. Their valor was as irresistible as their numbers were small. The Indians could in no wise resist their terrible onset, their war-cry doubly fierce from rage at the fate of their beloved king, who, to them, was, in truth, a demigod. They were driven from the spot, and Alexander was borne home to the camp. So enraged were the Macedonians at the wounding of their king, whom they believed to be mortally struck, that they spared neither man, woman, nor child in the town.

Alexander's wounds were indeed grave, but he recov-

ered, much to the joy of his army. While his life was de-
spaired of, a great deal of uncertainty and fear was engendered of their situation, for Alexander was the centre
around which revolved the entire mechanism. Without
him what could they do? How ever again reach their
homes? Every man believed that no one but the king
could lead them, and how much less in retreat than in
advance!

Alexander's fleet finally reached the mouth of the Indus.
The admiral, Nearchus, sailed to the Persian Gulf, while
Alexander and part of his army crossed the desert of Ge-
drosia, Craterus having moved by a shorter route with
another part and the invalids. When Alexander again
reached Babylon, his wonderful military career had ended.
In B.C. 323, he died there of a fever, and his great conquests and schemes of a Græco-Oriental monarchy were
dissipated.

Alexander was possessed of uncommon beauty. Plu-
tarch says that Lysippus made the best portrait of him,
"the inclination of the head a little on one side towards
the left shoulder, and his melting eye, having been expressed by this artist with great exactness." His likeness
was less fortunately caught by Apelles. He was fair and
ruddy, sweet and agreeable in person. Fond of study, he
read much history, poetry, and general literature. His
favorite book was the Iliad, a copy of which, annotated
by Aristotle, with a dagger, always lay under his pillow.
He was at all times surrounded by men of brains, and
enjoyed their conversation. He was abstinent of pleasures,
except drinking. Aristobulus says Alexander did not

drink much in quantity, but enjoyed being merry. Still, the Macedonian "much" was more than wisdom dictates. He had no weaknesses, except that he over-enjoyed flattery and was rash in temper.

Alexander was active, and able to endure heat and cold, hunger and thirst, trial and fatigue, beyond even the stoutest. He was exceeding swift of foot, but when young would not enter the Olympic games because he had not kings' sons to compete with. In an iron body dwelt both an intellect clear beyond compare, and a heart full of generous impulses. He was ambitious, but from high motives. His desire to conquer the world was coupled with the purpose of furthering Greek civilization. His courage was, both physically and morally, high-pitched. He actually enjoyed the delirium of battle, and its turmoils raised his intellect to its highest grade of clearness and activity. His instincts were keen; his perception remarkable; his judgment all but infallible. As an organizer of an army, unapproached; as a leader, unapproachable in rousing the ambition and courage of his men, and in quelling their fears by his own fearlessness. He kept his agreements faithfully. He was a remarkable judge of men. He had the rare gift of natural, convincing oratory, and of making men hang upon his lips as he spoke, and do deeds of heroism after. He lavished money rather on his friends than on himself.

While every inch a king, Alexander was friendly with his men; shared their toils and dangers; never asked an effort he himself did not make; never ordered a hardship of which he himself did not bear part. During the herculean pursuit of Darius, — after a march of four hundred miles in eleven days, on which but sixty of his men could keep beside him, and every one was all but dying of thirst, — when a helmetful of water was offered him, he declined to drink, as there was not enough for all. Such things endear a leader to his men beyond the telling. But Alexander's temper, by inheritance quick, grew ungovernable. A naturally excitable character, coupled with a certain superstitious tendency, was the very one to suffer from a life which carried him to such a giddy height, and from successes which reached beyond the human limit. We condemn, but, looking at him as a captain, may pass over those dark hours in his life which narrate the murder of Clitus, the execution of Philotas and Parmenio, and the cruelties to Bessus and to Batis. Alexander was distinctly subject to human frailties. His vices were partly inherited, partly the outgrowth of his youth and wonderful career. He repented quickly and sincerely of his evil deeds Until the last few years of his life his habits were very simple. His adoption then of Persian dress and manners was so largely a political requirement, that it can be hardly ascribed to personal motives, even if we fully acknowledge his vanity.

The life-work of Philip had been transcendant. That of Alexander surpasses anything in history. Words fail to describe the attributes of Alexander as a soldier. The perfection of all he did was scarcely understood by his historians. But to compare his deeds with those of other captains excites our wonder. Starting with a handful of men from Macedonia, in four years, one grand achievement after another, and without a failure, had placed at his feet the kingdom of the Great King. Leaving home with an enormous debt, in fifty moons he had possessed himself of all the treasures of the earth. Thence, with marvellous courage, endurance, intelligence, and skill he completed the conquest of the entire then known world, marching over nineteen thousand miles in his eleven years' campaigns. And all this before he was thirty-two. His health and strength were still as great as ever; his voracity for conquest greater, as well as his ability to conquer. It is an interesting question, had he not died, what would have become of Rome. The Roman infantry was as good as his; not so their cavalry. An annually elected consul could be no match for Alexander. But the king never met in his campaigns such an opponent as the Roman Republic, nor his phalanx such a rival as the Roman legion would have been. That was reserved for Hannibal.

Greek civilization, to a certain degree, followed Alexander's footsteps, but this was accidental. "You are a man like all of us, Alexander," said the naked Indian, "except that you abandon your home, like a meddlesome destroyer, to invade the most distant regions, enduring hardship yourself and inflicting it on others." Alexander could never have erected a permanent kingdom on his theory of coalescing races by intermarriages and forced migrations. His Macedonian-Persian Empire was a mere dream.

Alexander was never a Greek. He had but the Greek genius and intelligence grafted on the ruder Macedonian nature; and he became Asiaticized by his conquests. His life-work, as cut out by himself, was to conquer and then to Hellenize Asia. He did the one, he could not accomplish the other aim. He did not plant a true and permanent Hellenism in a single country of Asia. None of his cities have lived. They were rather fortified posts than self-sustaining marts. As a statesman, intellectual, far-seeing, and broad, he yet conceived and worked on an impossible theory, and the immediate result of all his genius did not last a generation.

What has Alexander done for the art of war? When Demosthenes was asked what were the three most important qualities in an orator, he replied : " Action, action, action ! " In another sense this might well be applied to the captain. No one can become a great captain without a mental and physical activity which are almost abnormal, and so soon as this exceptional power of activity wanes, the captain has come to a term of his greatness. Genius has been described as an extraordinary capacity for hard work. But this capacity is but the human element. Genius implies the divine spark. It is the personality of the great captain which makes him what he is. The maxims of war are but a meaningless page to him who cannot apply them. They are helpful just so far as the man's brain and heart, as his individuality, can carry them. It is because a great captain must first of all be a great man, and because to the lot of but few great men belongs the peculiar ability or falls the opportunity of being great captains, that preëminent success in war is so rarely seen.

All great soldiers are cousins-german in equipment of heart and head. No man ever was, no man can by any possibility blunder into being, a great soldier without the most generous virtues of the soul, and the most distinguished powers of the intellect. The former are independence, self-reliance, ambition within proper bounds ; that sort of physical courage which not only does not know fear, but which is not even conscious that there is such a thing as courage ; that greater moral quality which can hold the lives of tens of thousands of men and the destinies of a great country or cause patiently, intelligently, and unflinchingly in his grasp ; powers of endurance which cannot be overtaxed ; the unconscious habit of ruling men and of commanding their love and admiration, coupled with the ability to stir their enthusiasm to the yielding of their last ounce of effort. The latter comprise business capacity of the very highest order, essential to the care of his troops ; keen perceptions, which even in extraordinary circumstances or sudden emergencies are not to be led astray ; the ability to think as quickly and accurately in the turmoil of battle as in the quiet of the bureau ; the power to foresee to its ultimate conclusion the result of a strategic or tactical manœuvre ; the capacity to gauge the efforts of men and of masses of men ; the many-sidedness which can respond to the demands of every detail of the battle-field, while never losing sight of the one object aimed at ; the mental strength which weakens not under the tax of hours and days of unequalled strain. For, in truth, there is no position in which man can be placed which asks so much of his intellect in so short a space as that of the general, the failure or success, the decimation or security of whose army hangs on his instant thought and unequivocal instruction under the furious and kaleidoscopic ordeal of the field. To these qualities of heart and head add one factor more — opportunity — and you have the great soldier.

Now, Alexander was the first man, the details of whose history have been handed down to us, who possessed these qualities in the very highest measure; whose opportunities were coextensive with his powers; and who out of all these wrought a methodical system of warfare from which we may learn lessons to-day. Look at what he accomplished with such meagre means! He alone has the record of uniform success with no failure. And this, not because he had weak opponents, for while the Persians were far from redoubtable, except in numbers, the Tyrians, the tribes beyond the Caucasus, and the Indians, made a bold front and good fight.

Alexander's movements were always made on a well-conceived, maturely-digested plan; and this he kept in view to the end, putting aside all minor considerations for the main object, but never losing sight of these. His grasp was as large as his problem. His base for his advance into the heart of the then known world was the entire coast-line of the then known sea. He never advanced, despite his speed, without securing flanks and rear, and properly garrisoning the country on which he based. Having done this he marched on his objective, — which was wont to be the enemy's army, — with a directness which was unerring. His fertility in ruse and stratagem was unbounded. He kept well concentrated; his division of forces was always warranted by the conditions, and always with a view of again concentrating. His rapidity was unparalleled. It was this which gave him such an ascendant over all his enemies. Neither winter cold nor summer heat, mountain nor desert, the widest rivers nor the most elaborate defences, ever arrested his course ; and yet his troops were always well fed. He was a master of logistics. He lived on the country he campaigned in as entirely as Napoleon, but was careful to accumulate granaries in the most available places. He was remarkable in being able to keep the gaps in his army filled by recruits from home or enlistments of natives, and in transforming the latter into excellent soldiers. Starting from home with thirty-five thousand men, he had in the Indian campaigns no less than one hundred and thirty-five thousand, and their deeds proved the stuff that was in them.

Alexander's battles are tactically splendid examples of conception and execution. The wedge at Arbela was more splendid than Macdonald's column at Wagram. It was a scintillation of genius. Alexander saw where his enemy's strength and weakness lay, and took prompt advantage of them. He utilized his victories to the full extent, and pursued with a vigor which no other has ever reached. He was equally great in sieges as in battles. The only thing he was never called on to show was the capacity to face disaster. He possessed every remarkable military attribute; we can discover in him no military weakness.

As a captain, he accomplished more than any man ever did. He showed the world, first of all men, and best, how to make war. He formulated the first principles of the art, to be elaborated by Hannibal, Cæsar, Gustavus Adolphus, Frederick, and Napoleon. His conditions did not demand that he should approach to the requirements of modern war. But he was easily master of his trade, as, perhaps, no one else ever was. For, as Napoleon says, " to guess at the intentions of the enemy; to divine his opinion of yourself; to hide from him both your own intentions and opinion; to mislead him by feigned manœuvres; to invoke ruse, as well as digested schemes, so as to fight under the best conditions, — this is, and always was, the art of war."

LECTURE II.

HANNIBAL.

TWO generations after the death of Alexander, the power of the Mediterranean world was divided between Aryan Rome and Carthage, the vigorous daughter of Semitic Tyre. Carthage was first on the sea; Rome, on land. But Rome, always intolerant of powerful neighbors, fell to quarrelling with her great rival, and at the end of a twenty-three years' struggle, — the first Punic War, — imposed her own terms on defeated Carthage (241 B.C.). There were two parties bred of these hostilities in Carthage, — the war party, headed by Hamilcar Barca; the peace party, headed by Hanno. Hamilcar knew that peace with Rome meant oppression by Rome, and final extinction, and was ready to stake all on renewing the struggle. But he saw that present war was impossible; that opposition could only be in the future, and that it must be quietly prepared for. With a view of doing this, Hamilcar got the consent of the Carthaginian Senate to attempt the subjugation of Spain, a land of great natural resources, in conquering and holding which an army could be created which by and by might again cope with the Italian tyrant.

The Carthaginian fleet had been destroyed. Rome would not permit the building of a new one. Hamilcar's army was obliged to march overland from Carthage along the north coast of Africa and ship across the strait, — now Gibraltar. This was a bold thing to do, but it succeeded, and, in a series of campaigns, Hamilcar reduced the southern half of Spain, and (B.C. 236–227) firmly planted the Carthaginian power there. So conciliatory as well as vigorous had been his policy, that, on his death, the native tribes elected Hasdrubal, his son-in-law, general-in-chief of the allied Carthaginian and Spanish forces, which then amounted to nearly seventy thousand men and two hundred elephants.

Hasdrubal continued the policy of Hamilcar, and largely increased the Spanish influence and territory. But as Rome had colonies in northern Spain, the two powers were sure soon again to clash. In fact, Rome, after awhile, woke up to this new danger, and notified Carthage that she would extend her colonies north of the Ebro at her peril.

Hannibal was the son of Hamilcar. His father gave him the best Greek education, and this the lad's remarkable intellect readily assimilated. He trained him to arms under his own eye. Hannibal received his first schooling as a soldier at the age of nine, in his father's camps in Spain, and later his brother, Hasdrubal, made him his chief of calvary at the age of twenty-one. A pen-picture by Hannibal's arch enemy, Livy, tells us what he then was: "No sooner had he arrived than Hannibal drew the whole army towards him. The old soldiers fancied they saw

Hamilcar in his youth given back to them ; the same bright look, the same fire in his eye, the same trick of countenance and features.   But soon he proved that to be his father's son was not his highest recommendation.   Never was one and the same spirit more skilful to meet opposition, to obey or to command.   It was hard to decide whether he was more dear to the chief or the army.   Neither did Hasdrubal more readily place any one at the head when courage or activity was required, nor were the soldiers under any other leader so full of confidence and daring. He entered danger with the greatest mettle, he comported himself in danger with the greatest unconcern.   By no difficulties could his body be tired, his ardor damped. Heat and cold he suffered with equal endurance ; the amount of his food and drink was gauged by natural needs, and not by desire.   The time of waking and sleeping depended not on the distinction of day and night. What time was left from business he devoted to rest, and this was not brought on by either a soft couch or by quiet.   Many have often seen him covered by a short field-cloak lying on the ground betwixt the outposts and sentinels of the soldiers.   His clothing in no wise distinguished him from his fellows ; his weapons and horses attracted every one's eye.   He was by long odds the best rider, the best marcher.   He went into battle the first, he came out of it the last. . . . .   Hannibal served three years under Hasdrubal's supreme command, and left nothing unobserved which he who desires to become a great leader ought to see and to do."

Hannibal and his brothers had been brought up with an

intensity of hatred of Rome which it is hard to describe. Every schoolboy knows the anecdote of the lad's swearing never to make peace with Rome. The feeling grew with his years. When Hannibal was twenty-four, Hasdrubal died, and he himself was unanimously elected his successor.

Hamilcar had planned an invasion of Italy by way of the Alps; but the scheme was left inchoate at his death. Hannibal at once began definitely to pave the way for such an enterprise by completing the conquest of Spain. The original conception of crossing the Alps was Hamilcar's, just as Philip originally planned the invasion of Asia. But it was the fertile brain of Hannibal which gave the undertaking birth. The colossal nature of the plan, its magnificent daring, the boundless self-confidence and contempt of difficulty and danger which it implies, no less than the extraordinary manner of its execution, are equalled only by Alexander's setting forth — also but a lad — to conquer the illimitable possessions of the Great King.

In three years (B.C. 221–218) Hannibal had subjugated all Spain, and after a long siege captured Saguntum. He finally set out, with fifty thousand foot, nine thousand horse, and thirty-seven elephants, across the Pyrenees, whence his route was almost as unknown to him as the Atlantic to Columbus. It is impossible to follow him in this wonderful march, — the first crossing of the Alps by any but isolated merchants, — and probably the most daring enterprise ever set on foot. After toils and dangers impossible to gauge, even by the losses, Hannibal reached the Po in October, B.C. 218, with but twenty-six thousand men and a few elephants, less than half the force with which he had left Spain. With this handful he was to face a nation capable with its allies of raising seven hundred thousand men ; and yet the event — as well as our knowledge of Hannibal — shows that he had contemplated even this vast odds.

But Rome was not ready. Hannibal gained numberless confederates among the Gauls in northern Italy, and that same fall and winter won two victories over the Romans at the Ticinus and Trebia. Next year (B.C. 217) he again defeated the Romans, by an ambuscade at Lake Trasymene, killing or capturing their entire army of thirty thousand men. These three victories were due to the over-eagerness of the Roman generals to fight, their careless methods, and Hannibal's skill in handling his troops and his aptness at stratagem.

The campaign preceding, and the battle of Lake Trasymene, taught the Romans two valuable lessons. The instruction given the world by Alexander had not reached self-important, republican Rome, though Hannibal was familiar enough with the deeds of the great Macedonian. The Romans knew nothing of war except crude, hard knocks. The first lesson showed them that there is something in the art of war beyond merely marching out to meet your enemy and beating him by numbers, better weapons, or greater discipline.

It was thus : The Romans had retired into Etruria. In March, B.C. 217, Hannibal, who was in Liguria, desired to cross the Appenines and move upon them. There were but two roads he could pursue. The highway would

take him across the mountains, but by a long circuit.
This was the route by which the Consul Flaminius, at
Aretium, with his forty thousand men, was expecting him,
and, therefore, the way Hannibal did not choose to march,
for Flaminius could easily block the mountain roads. The
other route was so difficult that Flaminius never dreamed
that Hannibal knew of, or could by any possibility pursue

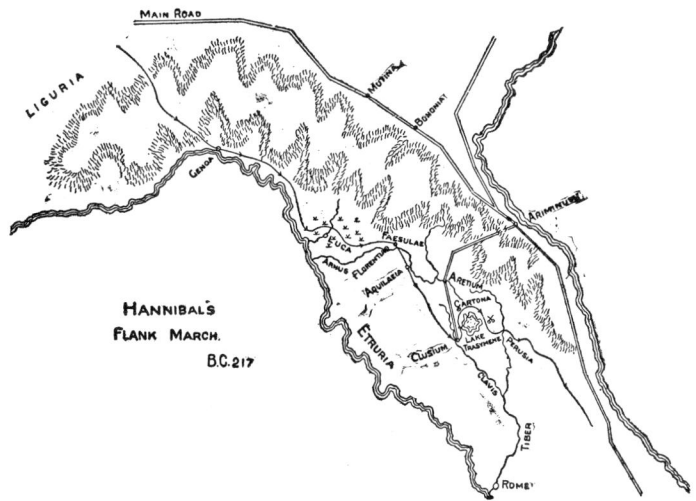

it. Hannibal's crossing of the Alps had taught Flaminius
nothing of his daring or his skill. This route lay along the
coast to near the mouth of the Arnus, and thence up the
right bank. It ran through an immense marsh, which, for
an army, was all but as difficult an obstacle as the Alps.
But it was the lesser evil, and promised the greater results ;
and Hannibal chose it, as Napoleon did the Great St.
Bernard in 1800. No better description of the task can
be given than to say that for four days and three nights

the army marched through water where only the wagons dead animals, or abandoned packs afforded the men any chance for rest. But the Carthaginian general reached his goal, turned Flaminius' left flank, and cut him off from Rome. Here was the conception of turning the enemy's strategic flank as clearly carried out as ever Napoleon did it. Such was lesson one.

The result of this turning manœuvre was the battle of Lake Trasymene, — where Hannibal taught the Romans, and us through them, the second lesson. The Romans had always marched in careless open order, without any idea of van or rear guard, or of flankers. This Hannibal knew. He placed his whole army in hiding at both ends of a defile at Lake Trasymene, through which the Romans must march, in such a manner that, when he made his attack, it was on an unsuspecting column, — in front, rear, and one flank; and the lake being on the other flank, the result was utter annihilation. After this the Romans marched with proper precautions. Hannibal had inflicted three staggering blows on his enemy.

But Rome now appointed a Dictator, — Quintus Fabius, — truly surnamed Maximus, and nicknamed Cunctator, because, recognizing that he was not able to cope with Hannibal on the battle-field, he wisely chose to conduct a campaign of delays and small war, the one thing Hannibal could not afford, but also the one thing the Romans could not tolerate or understand; for the Romans had always won by crisp fighting. Still, it was the policy shaped by Fabius which eventually defeated Hannibal, and next to

Hannibal himself, he was the best master the Romans then had.

It is impossible, even slightly, to touch on many of Hannibal's campaigns and battles. I prefer to give a short description of the battle of Cannæ, which, in its conduct and results, is typical of Hannibal's methods. And first, a few words about the organization of either army.

The Carthaginian discipline was based on the Macedonian idea, and the formation of the troops was phalangial, that is, in close masses. But Hannibal's army contained troops of all kinds, from the Numidian horseman, whose only clothing was a tiger-skin, on his tough little runt of a pony, or the all but naked Gaul with his long, curved sword, to the Carthaginian heavy-armed hypaspist. All these diverse tribes had each its own manner of fighting, and it required a Hannibal to keep up discipline or tactical efficiency in such a motley force. The Roman army, on the contrary, was wonderfully homogeneous, carefully disciplined, in all parts organized and drilled in the same manner, and the legion was a body which was the very opposite of the phalanx. It had much more mobility, the individual soldiers were more independent in action, and instead of relying on one shock or on defence, the several lines could relieve each other, and renew a failing battle three or even four times with fresh troops. After Trasymene, Hannibal not only armed his men with captured Roman weapons, but modified his organization somewhat to the legion pattern.

The legion was at this time formed in three lines of maniples (or companies) placed checkerwise. In front were the hastati, the least efficient; behind this the principes; and in the rear the triarii, or veterans. Each maniple was an excellent tactical unit. Each of these lines could relieve the other, and thus give a succession of hammer-like blows.

The phalanx we already know, and while it was wonderful for one shock, it had no reserve, and if demoralization set in, it was gone. The tendency of formation in ancient days, as now, was towards greater mobility, and later on the Roman legion in Greece, particularly at Pydna (168 B.C.), proved that it was superior, if properly handled, to the phalanx.

In B.C. 216, Æmilius Paulus and Varro were consuls. The former was a man of high character and attainments; Varro came of plebeian stock, was overbearing and self-sufficient. The Roman and Carthaginian armies lay facing each other near the Aufidus, Hannibal backing on Cannæ. His position here had been the result of an admirable manœuvre. The consuls commanded on alternate days. There had been a serious combat on the last day of Varro's command, in which the Carthaginians had been outnumbered two to one, and been defeated. This had greatly elated Varro, and whetted his appetite for battle. He left the troops at evening in such a manner that next day his associate was badly placed. Æmilius scarcely wished to withdraw, lest his men should be disheartened; he could not remain where he was, as he was exposed to Hannibal's better cavalry. He took a middle course, on the whole unwise. He sent a third of his force to the north of the Aufidus, a trifle up-stream, to sustain some foragers he had there, and make a secondary camp, from which to annoy

Hannibal's parties in search of corn. This division of forces was very risky. Hannibal had long been trying to bring the consuls to battle, and now saw that the moment had come, for Varro was precipitate, and would probably draw Æmilius into active measures.

Each general made a stirring address to his army. Polybius gives both. Hannibal's has the true ring of the great captain. " Let us hasten into action. I promise

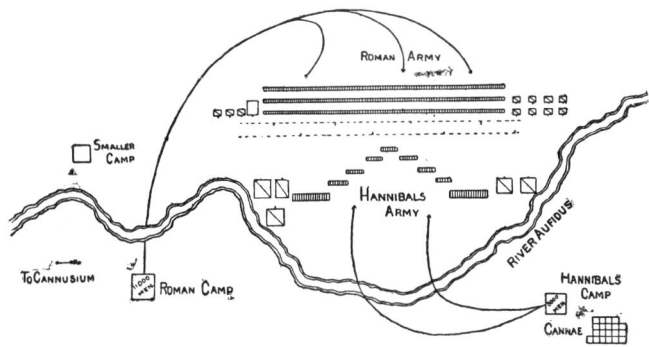

BATTLE OF CANNAE. B.C. 216
1

you victory, and, the gods willing, I will make my promise good." Two days later Hannibal offered Æmilius battle. But Æmilius declined it, and Hannibal sent his Numidians to the other side to annoy the Roman foragers. The succeeding day, knowing Varro to be in command, Hannibal again offered battle, aware that the hot-tempered Roman would be burning to avenge the yesterday's taunt. He left eight thousand men to guard his camp.

There has been much discussion as to which bank of the Aufidus was the scene of the battle. It seems to me that the plan in the diagram comes nearest to fitting all the statements, however conflicting, of the several authorities. Near Hannibal's camp the Aufidus makes a bold, southerly sweep. Here Hannibal forded the stream in two columns, drew up his army, and leaned his flanks on the river-banks so as to prevent the Romans, with their numerical superiority, from overlapping them. His front he covered with archers and slingers, so as to hide his formation from the Roman generals. Varro, as Hannibal anticipated, thought the Carthaginians were crossing to attack the lesser camp, and leaving eleven thousand men to guard the larger one, with orders to attack Hannibal's camp during the battle, he also crossed and drew up in the plain opposite the Carthaginians, he and every Roman in the ranks craving to come to blows with the hated invaders.

Varro also threw out his light troops in advance. He had sixty-five thousand foot and seven thousand horse, to Hannibal's thirty-two thousand foot and ten thousand horse. He could not overlap Hannibal's flanks, so he determined to make his line heavier, and seek to crush him at the first impact. He changed the formation of the maniples so as to make them sixteen men deep and ten men front, instead of sixteen men front by ten deep, as usual. This was a grievous error. His men were unapt to manœuvre or fight well in this unwonted form. He should have employed his surplus, say twenty-five thousand men, as a reserve for emergencies. His army was in the usual three lines, fifteen legions in all, the Roman on the right, the allied on the left. The intervals between the maniples always equalled their front, and the distance between the lines the depth of the maniples. The Roman cavalry, twenty-four hundred strong, was on the right. The allied, forty-eight hundred strong, on the left. It would have been better massed in one body. But such was the only formation then known. Æmilius commanded the right, Varro the left wing.

Hannibal placed on his left, opposite the Roman cavalry, his heavy Spanish and Gallic horse, eight thousand strong, two-thirds in a first, and one-third in a second line. This body was strong enough to crush the Roman horse, and thus cut off the retreat of the legions to their camps and towards Rome. In other words, Hannibal's fighting was to be forced on the Romans' strategic flank. He had a perfectly lucid idea of the value of a blow from this direction. On his right, facing the allied cavalry, were his Numidians, two thousand strong. Of the infantry, the Spaniards and Gauls were in the centre in alternate bodies. His best troops, the African foot, he placed on their either flank. He expected these veterans to leaven the whole lump. The foot was all in phalanxes of one thousand and twenty-four men each, the African foot in sixteen ranks, as usual, the Spaniards and Gauls in ten. Hannibal had been obliged thus to make his centre thin, from lack of men, but he had seething in his brain a manœuvre by which he proposed to make this very weakness a factor of success. He had been on the ground and had seen Varro strengthen the Roman centre. This confirmed him in his plan.

Hannibal commanded the centre in person, Hanno the right, Hasdrubal the left, Maharbal the cavalry of the left.

Hannibal relied on Maharbal to beat the Roman cavalry, and then, riding by the rear of the Roman army, to join the Numidians on the Carthaginian right, like Coenus at the Hydaspes. His cavalry was superior in numbers, and vastly outranked in effectiveness the Roman horse.

Hannibal was, no doubt, familiar with Marathon. He proposed to better the tactics of that day. Remember that Miltiades had opposed to him Orientals; Hannibal faced Roman legions. His general plan was to withdraw his centre before the heavy Roman line, — to allow them to push it in, — and then to enclose them in his wings and fall on their flanks. This was a highly dangerous manœuvre, unless the withdrawal of the centre could be checked at the proper time; but his men had the greatest confidence in him; the river in his rear would be an aid, if he could but keep his men steady; and in war no decisive result can be compassed without corresponding risk. Hannibal had fully prepared his army for this tactical evolution, and rehearsed its details with all his subordinates. He not only had the knack of making his lieutenants comprehend him, but proposed to see to the execution of the work himself.

The Carthaginians faced north, the Romans south. The rising sun was on the flank of either. The wind was southerly, and blew the dust into the faces of the Romans. The light troops on either side opened the action, and fiercely contested the ground for some time. During the preliminary fighting, Hannibal advanced his centre, the Spanish and Gallic foot, in a salient or convex order from the main line, the phalanxes on the right and left of the central one being, it is presumed, in *echelon* to it. The wings, of African foot, kept their place.

While this was being done, Hannibal ordered the heavy horse on his left to charge down on the Roman horse in their front. This they did with their accustomed spirit, but met a gallant resistance. The Roman knights fought for every inch with the greatest obstinacy, when dismounted, continuing the contest on foot. The fighting was not by shocks, it was rather hand to hand. But the weight and superior training of the Carthaginian horse soon told. They rode down the Romans and crushed them out of existence. Æmilius was badly wounded, but escaped the ensuing massacre and made his way to the help of the Roman centre, hoping there to retrieve the day. On the Carthaginian right the Numidians had received orders to skirmish with the allied horse and not come to a decisive combat till they should be joined by the heavy horse from the Carthaginian left. This they did in their own peculiar style, by riding around their opponents, squadron by squadron, and by making numberless feigned attacks. The battle in the centre had not yet developed results, when Maharbal, having destroyed the Roman cavalry, and ridden around the Roman army, appeared in the rear of the allied horse. The Numidians now attacked seriously, and between them, in a few minutes, there was not a Roman horseman left upon the field alive. The Numidians were then sent in pursuit, Maharbal remaining upon the field.

While this was going on, the light troops of both sides had been withdrawn through the intervals, and had

formed in the rear and on the flanks of legion and phalanx, ready to fill gaps and supply the heavy foot with
weapons. This had uncovered Hannibal's salient. Varro
had committed still another blunder. In the effort to
make his line so strong as to be irresistible, he had ordered
his maniples of principes from the second line forward
into the intervals of the maniples of hastati in first line,
thus making one solid wall and robbing the legionaries of
their accustomed mobility, as well as lending them a feeling of uncertainty in their novel formation. Still, with its
wonted spirit, the heavy Roman line advanced on Hannibal's salient. The Carthaginian wings could not yet be
reached, being so much refused. Striking the apex, the
fighting became furious. Hannibal's salient, as proposed,
began to withdraw, holding its own in good style. Varro,
far too eager, and seeing, as he thought, speedy victory
before him, was again guilty of the folly of ordering the
third line, the triarii, and even the light troops, up to the
support of the already overcrowded first and second lines.
The Carthaginian centre, supported by its skirmishers, held
the ground with just enough tenacity to whet the determination of the Romans to crush it. Varro now insanely
ordered still more forces in from his wings to reënforce
his centre, already a mass so crowded as to be unable to
retain its organization, but pressing back the Carthaginians by mere weight of mass. He could not better have
played into Hannibal's hands. The Romans — three men
in the place of one — struggled onward, but became every
moment a more and more jumbled body. Its maniple
formation, and consequent ease of movement, was quite

lost. Still, it pushed forward, as if to certain victory, and still the Carthaginian salient fell back, till from a salient it became a line, from a line a reëntering angle or crescent. Hannibal, by great personal exertions, had in an extraor·· dinary manner preserved the steadiness and formation of his centre, though outnumbered four to one. The Car·· thaginian wings he now ordered slowly to advance, which all the more edged the Roman centre into the *cul-de-sac*

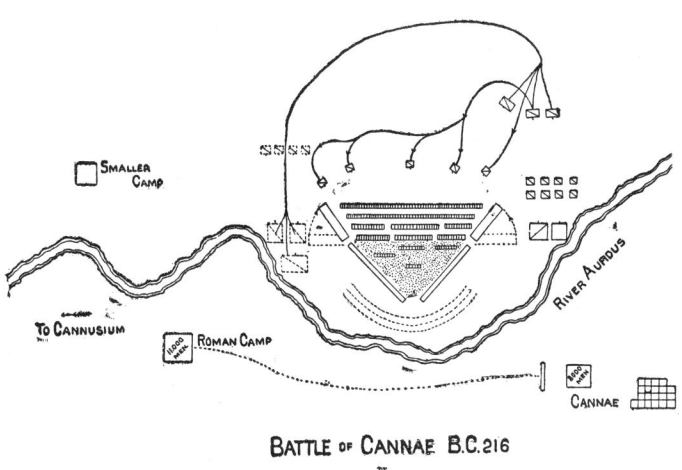

BATTLE ᴏꜰ CANNAE B.C. 216
II.

Hannibal had prepared. The Roman legionaries were already shouting their eager cry of victory; but so herded together had they got that there was no room to use their weapons. Hannibal had kept the Carthaginian centre free from any feeling of demoralization, and ready at his com-mand to turn and face the enemy. The wings, by their advance, had hustled the Roman legions into the form of a wedge without a vestige of maniple formation left. The decisive moment had come. Hannibal seized it with the eye of the born soldier. Arresting the backward movement of the centre, which still had elbow-room to fight, as the Romans had not, he gave the orders to the wings which they were impatiently awaiting. These veteran troops, in perfect order, wheeled inward to right and left, on the flanks of the struggling mass of legionaries. The Roman army was lost beyond a ray of hope, for, at the same instant, Maharbal, having finished the destruction of the cavalry, rode down upon its rear. The cry of victory changed to a cry of terror. Defeat degenerated into mere slaughter. The Carthaginian cavalry divided into small troops and rode into the midst of the Roman soldiers, sabring right and left. Some squadrons galloped around to the flanks and lent a hand to the African phalanx in its butchery. No quarter was given, or indeed asked. The Romans died with their faces to the foe. The bloody work continued till but a handful was left. Livy and Polybius place the killed at from forty to seventy thousand men. Varro had already escaped with a mere squad of horse. Æmilius Paullus died, sword in hand, seeking to stem the tide of disaster. Three pro-consuls, two quæstors, twenty-one military tribunes, a number of ex-consuls, prætors, and ædiles, and eighty senators, perished with the army.

Hannibal's loss had been barely six thousand men, but he had annihilated the splendid army of eighty-seven thousand men — the flower of Rome. It had vanished as if swallowed up in an earthquake. The battle had been won by crisp tactical skill and the most effective use of cavalry, — as fine as that at the Hydaspes. It was, indeed, the gorgeous handling of the cavalry which made the infantry manœuvre possible.

Few battles in history are more marked by ability on the one side and crass blundering on the other than the battle of Cannæ. The handling of the cavalry was quite beyond praise. The manner in which the far from reliable Spanish and Gallic foot was advanced in a wedge in *echelon*, and, under the mettlesome attack of the Roman legions, was first held there, and then withdrawn step by step, until it had reached the converse position of a reëntering angle, and was then steadied in place by ordering up the light troops into its intervals, — all this being done under the exultant Roman shouts of victory, — is a simple *chef d'œuvre* of battle-tactics, due solely to Hannibal's magnificent personality ; and the advance at the decisive instant of the African infantry, and its wheel right and left upon the flanks of the disordered and overcrowded legionaries, caps the master-stroke. The whole battle, from the Carthaginian stand-point, is a consummate piece of art, having no superior, few equals in the history of war.

It is usual for historians to blame Hannibal for not at once marching on Rome after this victory. Let us see what his chances were. We have no hint of what he himself thought, of what his reasons were for not so doing. We must content ourselves with collecting a few guess-work items, and endeavoring to argue as he did.

Two facts are peculiarly prominent in Hannibal's campaign in Italy. First, he had opposed to him the troops of the strongest and most intelligent military power of the world, some of which were, to be sure, comparatively raw in active duty, but yet trained to war from their youth, mixed with legionaries of many campaigns, and instinct with the ardor of fighting for their household gods. It is often assumed that Hannibal's troops were veterans, the Romans levies of a day. During the first three years this was in part true, and defeat had somewhat drawn the temper of the Roman blade; but throughout the rest of Hannibal's campaigns the Roman army was much superior to his own in all but one quality, — that strange influence which a great man exercises over men. It will be noticed that whenever the fighting was on equal terms, from the beginning the Roman soldier gave a good account of himself. But Hannibal's victories were won by stratagem, or by tactical genius and skilful use of his cavalry arm, not by brute fighting. In the latter act the legionary was fully the equal of the phalangite. One cannot compare the task of any other great captain with that of Hannibal. No one ever faced such odds. Secondly, Hannibal had calculated absolutely upon being able to detach the allies — the socii — from their fealty. We cannot imagine him to have set out on his marvellous expedition without having made this the prime factor in his calculations. Hannibal was no madman. He was a keen, close calculator. But he would have been insane, indeed, if he had undertaken his hazardous campaign without such expectation. He was well justified in reckoning on such defection. There had always been a good deal of opposition to high-handed Rome among all her allies, municipal cities, and colonies, and it was a fair assumption that many, if not most, of them would be glad to free themselves and humble their proud conqueror and mistress. In this expectation Hannibal had been entirely disappointed. None of the socii, who were the brawn of the Roman body, had shown any disposition to meet him otherwise than with the sword; none of the colonies, except in distant Gaul, had met him even half way. He had captured towns and territory and had garrisoned citadels. But the aid he received was not that which enables a conqueror to hold what he takes except with the strong hand. And without just such aid, Hannibal could not only not win, but could not be otherwise than defeated, in his contest with the mighty republic. To assume that Hannibal did not see all this, and that he was not fighting against hope almost from the second year, is to underrate this man's intellectual ability. No one ever fathomed Hannibal's purpose. He was so singularly reticent that Roman historians called him perfidious, because no one could, from his face or conduct, gauge either his thought or intention, or calculate upon his acts. He had no Hephæstion as had Alexander. But no doubt he was keenly alive to the failure, so far, of his calculation on the disaffection of the allies.

And now, after the overwhelming victory of Cannæ, he had to weigh not only the strategic and tactical difficulties, but the still more serious political ones. If the allies, or a good part of them, could be induced to join his cause, Rome would fall sooner or later. If not, he could never take Rome, nor permanently injure the Roman cause. The chances were, in a military sense, all against his capturing Rome by a *coup de main*. Rome was over two hundred miles distant, well walled, and with a large force which could be quickly gathered to protect it. If he failed, the game was lost. It was far wiser for him to still try to influence the allies, which he could now do with a record of wonderful victories such as the world had not yet seen. Hannibal was not a military gambler. He never risked his all on a bare chance, as some other soldiers have done. He always reckoned his chances closely. And every reason prompted him not to risk the loss of his all on the chances of a brilliant march on the enemy's capital, which had only its boldness to commend it, and every military reason as well as the stanch Roman heart to promise failure as its result; for there was no obsequious satrap to open its gates and welcome the conquering hero, as it had been Alexander's fortune to meet. If Hannibal marched on Rome, he must be prepared to besiege the city; and he had neither siege equipment, nor were sieges consonant with his peculiar ability. If the story be true that Maharbal asked of Hannibal, after Cannæ, that he might march on Rome with five thousand horse, promising that he should sup in the Capitol in four days, and that on Hannibal's declining, Maharbal exclaimed, " Truly, Hannibal, thou knowest how to win a victory, but knowest not how to use one !" it may tend to show that Maharbal possessed indeed the daring recklessness of a true general of cavalry, but it also proves that Hannibal had the discretion, as he had shown in abundant measure the enterprise, of the great captain.

Hannibal probably at this time harbored the hope that, after this fourth and overwhelming defeat of the Ro-

mans, the allies would finally see that their interests lay
with him. In fact, Capua, the Samnites, Lucanians, and
many cities of Lower Italy did join his cause, and the
unexplained time which he spent in the vicinity of his
late battle-field was no doubt devoted to political questions,
the favorable solution of which could be better brought
about by not for the moment risking his now unques-
tioned military supremacy.

The institutions and laws which gave Rome strength
never demonstrated her greatness so well as now. The
people which had created these institutions, which had
made these laws, never rose superior to disaster, never
exhibited the strength of character of which the whole
world bears the impress, so well as now. The horrible
disaster to both state and society — for there was not a
house in which there was not one dead — by no means
changed the determination of the Roman people, however horrified the cool-headed, however frightened the
many. Not that among the ignorant there was not fear
and trembling; but it was not the ignorant who had made
or ruled Rome. The more intelligent and courageous
element spoke with a single voice. The prætors at
once called the Senate together to devise means of defence, and it remained in constant session. All Rome
was in affliction, but this must not interfere with the necessity of saving the city, and courage must be outward
as well as in the heart. The word *peace* was forbidden
to be pronounced. Mourning was limited to thirty days.
Tears were prohibited to women in public. New energies were at once put at work. In view of the

alarming circumstances and the impossibility of carrying out the requirements of the law, the Senate itself made M. Junius Pera dictator, who chose Titus Sempronius Gracchus as master of cavalry. The entire male population above seventeen years of age was enrolled. Four new legions and one thousand horse were added to the city garrison. All mechanics were set to work to repair weapons. The walls were already in a state of excellent defence. The Senate purchased and armed eight thousand slaves and four thousand debtors or criminals, with promise of freedom and pardon. Naught but stubborn resistance to the last man was thought of. It was indeed well that Hannibal did not march on Rome.

Cannæ was the last great victory of Hannibal, but the beginning of his most masterly work. He had up to this moment conducted a brilliant offensive. There is nothing in the annals of war which surpasses his crossing of the Alps, his victories at the Ticinus and Trebia, his march through the Arnus marshes, his victory at Lake Trasymene, his manœuvres up to Cannæ, and that wonderful battle. But this splendid record had not helped his cause. Yet, against all hope, he stuck to his task for thirteen long years more, waiting for reënforcements from Carthage, or for some lucky accident which might turn the tide in his favor. Up to Cannæ Fortune had smiled upon him. After Cannæ she turned her back on him, never again to lend him aid.

Livy asserts that Hannibal's want of success came from his exposing his troops to a winter in Capua, where debauch destroyed their discipline. Many historians have followed this theory. But the soldier who looks at the remarkable work done by Hannibal from this time on, knows that nothing short of the most exemplary discipline can possibly account for it, and seeks his reasons elsewhere. Livy's statements will bear watching.

Hannibal soon became too weak to afford the attrition of great battles. He had sought to impose on the allies by brilliant deeds. He had failed, and must put into practice whatever system would best carry out his purpose. From this time on he avoided fighting unless it was forced upon him, but resorted to manœuvring to accomplish his ends. He seized important towns, he marched on the Roman communications, he harassed the enemy with small war. He did the most unexpected and surprising things. He appeared at one end of southern Italy before the enemy had any idea that he had left the other. He was teaching the Romans the trade of war. They were not slow to see wherein Hannibal's superiority lay, and profited by it. He educated their best generals, and these now came to the front.

The Romans raised annually from one hundred and fifty thousand to two hundred and forty thousand men, of which one-half to two-thirds were in Hannibal's own front, and they were of the bone and sinew of Rome. He himself never had more than thirty-five thousand to forty thousand effective, and these far from as good. The Carthaginian Senate, under lead of the Hanno faction, forsook him, nor sent him men nor money, except one small reënforcement. He was cast on his own resources in the enemy's country. While the Roman legions grew in numbers and experience, his own veterans gradually disappeared and left but a ragged force behind. And yet, during most of this time, he marched over the length and breadth of Italy, ravaging and destroying, and not one nor all the Roman armies could prevent him from acting out his pleasure.

Among all the brilliant lessons in strategy which Hannibal gave the Romans, there is time but to mention one more. Capua, one of the large cities of Italy, had embraced Hannibal's cause as the coming man. But Hannibal had — in B.C. 211—been crowded back into southern Italy, and the Romans were besieging Capua. He was called upon for aid. The Capuans were in sorry plight. Hannibal, who was blockading the citadel at Tarentum, left this pressing affair to answer their appeal, made a secret forced march, eluding the four consular legions in Apulia and at Beneventum, and suddenly appeared before the astonished Roman army at Capua, — intent on raising the siege. The Capuans and Carthaginians attacked the Roman lines at the same time, but both recoiled from superior numbers and entrenched position. Hannibal, seeing that he could not raise the siege by direct means, tried, for the first time in the history of strategy, an indirect means, hoping to effect by moral weight what he could not by weight of men. He marched straight on Rome. He counted on the proconsuls, from fear for their capital, to raise the siege of Capua and follow him. He knew he could not capture Rome, where were forces much larger than his own. But he ravaged the land to its very gates and filled the city with affright. Hannibal had, however, taught his pupils much too well. Rome was

terribly demoralized, and called lustily for the proconsuls'
armies to come from Capua to its aid. But these generals were not to be misled; they by no means relaxed
their grip, and Hannibal lost the game. At an earlier
stage of the war this brilliant movement would certainly
have raised the siege of Capua.

Finally, Hannibal became so reduced in numbers that he

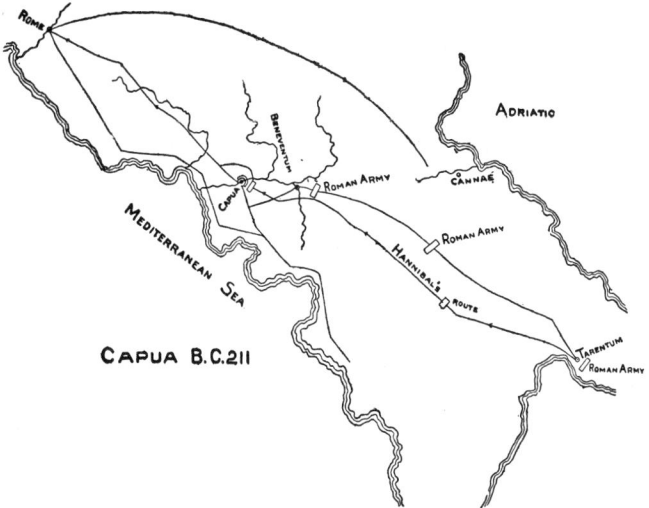

CAPUA B.C.211

was compelled to remain in the extreme south of Italy.
He could not move out of Brutium. His forces were
quite unequal to fighting, or even campaigning. He was
hoping against hope for some kind of recognition from
home, some aid in men and material. He could undertake
nothing, but clung to what he held with a despairing grasp.
Weak as he was, however, no Roman consul chose to come
within reach of his arm. His patience and constancy
under these trials, and the dread his name still inspired,

show him up in far greater measure than any of his tri
umphs. Even Livy, who is full of depreciation of Hannibal's abilities, says, "The Romans did not provoke him
while he remained quiet, such power did they consider that
single general possessed, though everything else around
him was falling into ruin," and is compelled to follow up
this statement with a panegyric.

For a dozen years Hannibal had held more or less territory in the midst of the Roman Empire, far from home and
his natural base. His old army had quite disappeared, and
a motley array of the most heterogeneous materials had
taken its place. He had for three or four years past had
nothing which he could oppose to the Roman legions without danger of — without actual defeat. His troops had
often neither pay nor clothing ; rations were scant ; their arms
were far from good ; they must have foreseen eventual disaster, as did Hannibal. And yet the tie between leader and
men never ceased to hold ; the few soldiers he had were all
devotion to his cause. Driven into a corner where he
must subsist his army on a limited area, which he could
only hold by forcing under his standard every man possibly
fit for service ; among a people whose greed for gold and
plunder was their chief characteristic, — he was still able not
only to keep his phalanxes together, but to subject them to
excellent discipline. The Carthaginians, meanwhile, were
only dreaming of holding on to Spain ; their one useful
captain, with all his possibilities, they were blindly neglecting. He was left absolutely to his own resources.
And yet, — it is so wonderful that one can but repeat it
again and again, — though there were several armies of

Roman veteran legions — for nearly all Roman soldiers were veterans now — around him on every side, such was the majesty which hedged his name, that neither one singly, nor all together, dared to come to the final conflict with him, brave and able though their leaders were. Even after the Metaurus, when the Romans knew what the effect of his brother's defeat must be on the *morale* of Hannibal's army, if not on himself, this dread of the very name of Hannibal, even by the best of the Roman generals, is almost inexplicable. They must each and all have recognized that it needed but one joint effort to crush out his weakened and depleted semblance of an army, and yet none of them was apparently willing to undertake the task. Whatever the Roman historians may tell us about these years, is not here really a great and stubborn fact, which testifies to more than a thousand pages penned by his detractors?

Finally, long after Hasdrubal had made his way to Italy, and had been defeated by the consul Nero, Rome carried the war into Africa, and Hannibal was recalled from Italy and defeated at Zama by Scipio. It was, however, neither Scipio nor Zama that defeated Hannibal. The Carthaginian cause had been doomed years before. It was inanition, pure and simple, which brought Hannibal's career to a close, — the lack of support of the Carthaginian Senate. He all but won Zama, even with the wretched material he had brought from Italy, and without cavalry, against the best army Rome had so far had, the most skilful general, and every fair chance. Had he won Zama, he must have lost the next battle. The Semitic cause against the Aryan was bound to fail.

This battle ended the war. Hannibal lived nineteen years after the defeat, for six years in Carthage, — thirteen in exile. Rome never felt secure until his death.

Hannibal ranks with the few great captains of the world. Alexander, Cæsar, Gustavus Adolphus, Frederick, Napoleon, alone can stand beside him. In this galaxy the stars are equal. His self-reliant courage, which prompted him to undertake the conquest of Italy with twenty thousand foot and six thousand horse, without a definite base, and with uncertain confederates, is the mark which stamps the genius — or the fool. Without the ability and iron resolution to do so vast a thing, no great man ever accomplished results. Upon such a rock have been shattered many reputations.

Hannibal had remarkable control over men. Reaching Cisalpine Gaul, it was but a few weeks before the whole province became his sworn allies, and they remained true and faithful to his cause, and bore their heavy burden with cheerful alacrity, — though then, as now, the most unstable of peoples. Hannibal possessed a keen knowledge of human nature, as well as an unbounded individual power over men. Unfortunately, only a few anecdotes remain to us as the portrait of this extraordinary man ; but we cannot doubt that he carried that personal magnetism with him which lent a wonderful strength to what he said or did.

His victories were as brilliant as any ever won ; but on these does not rest his chief glory. When he won Trebia, Trasymene, Cannæ, he had opposed to him generals ignorant of the art of war, which art the genius of Hannibal enabled him to use in a manner beyond all others, and which his experience in many arduous campaigns had taught him to the bottom. But Hannibal instructed these same Romans in this very art of war, — and his later opponents fought him on his own system, and with wonderful aptness at learning what he had instilled into them with such vast pains. These scholars of Hannibal, however, able as they became, never in any sense grew to their master's stature. They were strong in numbers and courage, they surrounded him on all sides, they cut off his reënforcements and victuals, they harassed his outposts and foragers, they embarrassed his marches, — all in the superb style he had shown them how to use. But, for all that, though outnumbering him many to one, not one or several of them could ever prevent his coming or going, at his own good time or pleasure, whithersoever he listed, and never was more than a momentary advantage gained over him in a pitched battle till the fatal day of Zama. Even after Hasdrubal's death, his aggressors dared not attack him. Like a pack of bloodhounds around the boar at bay, none ventured to close in on him for a final struggle. Even when he embarked for Carthage, — the most dangerous of operations possible for an army, — it was not attempted to hamper his progress. Even Scipio, in Italy, seemed by no means anxious to encounter him, — except at a disadvantage, — and in Africa did not meet him until he could do so on his own conditions, and under the very best of auspices.

By some, Scipio has been thought equal to Hannibal. But great soldier as Scipio was, he falls very far short of the rank attained by Hannibal. The list of generals of a lesser grade numbers many great names, among them that of Scipio, linked with commanders like Brasidas, Epaminondas, Xenophon, Prince Eugene, Turenne, Marlborough, Montecuculi. But between these and men of the stamp of Hannibal there is a great gulf fixed.

Like all great captains, Hannibal not infrequently violated what we now call the maxims of war; but when he did so, it was always with that admirable calculation of the power or weakness of the men and forces opposed to him, which, of itself, is the excuse for the act by that man who is able to take advantage of as well as to make circumstances. All great captains have a common likeness in this respect.

Napoleon aptly says: "The principles of Cæsar were the same as those of Alexander or Hannibal: to hold his forces in hand; to be vulnerable on several points only when it is unavoidable; to march rapidly upon the important points; to make use to a great extent of all moral means, such as the reputation of his arms, the fear he inspires, the political measures calculated to preserve the attachment of allies, and the submission of conquered provinces."

Such men have used the maxims of war only so far as they fitted into their plans and combinations. Success justifies them, but the failure of the lesser lights who infringe these maxims only proves them to be maxims indeed.

What has Hannibal done for the art of war? First and foremost he taught the Romans what war really is; that there is something beyond merely marching out, fighting a battle, and marching home again. He showed them that with but a small part of their numerical force, with less good material, with less good arms, with but a few allies, he could keep Rome on the brink of ruin and despair for two-thirds of a generation. He showed them for thirteen years that he could accomplish more than they could, despite their numbers, and without battle. And while battle should be always the legitimate outcome of all military manœuvres, Hannibal taught the Romans that there was something far higher in war than mere brute weight, and through the Romans he has taught us.

Hannibal was as typically a fighter as even Alexander, though he preferred to prescribe his own time and conditions. But all through Alexander's campaigns it happened that the results he aimed at could be accomplished only by hammering. And he had the power to hammer. Hannibal, on the contrary, found that he could not stand attrition; that he must save men. Alexander was constantly seeking conquests; Hannibal, like Frederick, only to keep what he had won, and in doing this he showed the world the first series of examples of intellectual war. Alexander's strategy, in its larger aspect, was as far-seeing and far-reaching as that of any of the great captains, and he was the first to show it. But Alexander's strategic movements had not been understood, and ran danger of being lost. Hannibal was, probably, the only man who understood what Alexander had done, and he impressed his own strategy so thoroughly upon the Romans that it modified their whole method of waging war. Alexander's strategy was equally marked. Like Cæsar's, his strategic field was the whole known world. But he did not exhibit that more useful phase of strategy, on a smaller theatre, which Hannibal has given us.

While Hannibal's movement into Italy was offensive, the years after Cannæ partook largely of the defensive. He was holding his own till he could get reënforcements from home, or the help of the Roman allies. And yet it was he who was the main-spring which furnished the action, the centre about which everything revolved. Perhaps there is no surer test of who is the foremost soldier of a campaign than to determine who it is upon whose action everything waits ; who it is that forces the others to gauge their own by his movements. And this Hannibal always did. It made no odds whether it was in his weak or his strong years. It was Hannibal's marching to and fro, Hannibal's manœuvres, offensive or defensive, which predetermined the movements of the Roman armies.

We know little about the personal appearance of Hannibal. We only know that in the march through the Arnus swamps he lost an eye. In the British Museum is an ancient bust of a soldier with but one eye — by some supposed to be Hannibal. But there is no authentic likeness of the man. It is improbable that he possessed Alexander's charm of beauty. But in all his other qualities, mental and physical, he was distinctly his equal ; and in his life he was simple, pure and self-contained.

Alexander did brilliant things for their own sake. Hannibal always forgot self in his work. Alexander needed adulation. Hannibal was far above such weakness. Alexander was open, hasty, violent. His fiery

nature often ran away with his discretion. Hannibal was
singularly self-poised. From his face you could never
divine his thought or intention. So marked was this
ability to keep his own counsel, never to betray his purpose, that the Roman historians talked of deception when
he did unexpected things. But Punic faith was distinctly
as good as Roman faith. The Romans promised and did
not perform; Hannibal never promised. Hannibal's mind
was broad, delicate, clear. His Greek training made him
intellectually the superior of any of the Roman generals.
His conception of operations and discrimination in means
were equalled by his boldness — even obstinacy — of execution.

Hannibal's influence over men is perhaps his most
wonderful trait. Alexander commanded fealty as a king,
as well as won it as a man; Hannibal earned the fidelity
and love of his men by his personal qualities alone.
When we consider the heterogeneous elements of which
his army was composed, the extraordinary hardships it
underwent, the hoping against hope, the struggling against
certain defeat and eventual annihilation, the toils and
privation, and remember that there was never a murmur
in his camp, or a desertion from his ranks, and that eventually he was able to carry his army, composed almost
entirely of Italians, over to Africa on the most dangerous
of tasks, and to fight them as he did at Zama, it may
be said that Hannibal's ability to keep this body together
and fit for work shows the most wonderful influence over
men ever possessed by man.

Alexander always had luck running in his favor. Hannibal is essentially the captain of misfortune. Alexander was always victorious ; Hannibal rarely so in battle in the last twelve years in Italy. Alexander fought against a huge but unwieldy opponent, brave, but without discipline, and top-heavy. Hannibal's work was against the most compact and able nation of the world, at its best period, the very type of a fighting machine. Not that all this in any sense makes Hannibal greater than Alexander, but it serves to heighten the real greatness of Hannibal.

Hannibal's marches were quick, secret, crafty. He was singularly apt at guessing what his enemy would do, and could act on it with speed and effect. He was unsurpassed in logistics. The Romans learned all they ever knew of this branch of the art from Hannibal. Despite the tax upon him, his men always had bread. He utilized his victories well, but was not led astray by apparent though delusive chances. As a besieger Hannibal was not Alexander's equal. Only Demetrius and Cæsar, perhaps, were. In this matter Hannibal and Frederick were alike. Both disliked siege-work.

But as a man, so far as we can know him, — and if he had any vices, his enemies, the Roman historians, would have dilated upon them, — Hannibal was perhaps, excepting Gustavus Adolphus, the most admirable of all. As a captain he holds equal rank with the others. As a distinguishing mark, we may well call him " The Father of Strategy."

LECTURE III.

CÆSAR.

CAIUS JULIUS CÆSAR is the only one of the great captains who trained himself to arms. Alexander, Hannibal, Gustavus Adolphus, Frederick, owed their early military training to their fathers, though, indeed, Frederick's was but the pipe-clay of war. Napoleon got his in the best school in France. Every Roman citizen was, to be sure, trained as a soldier, and Cæsar had had a slight experience in some minor campaigns. But the drilling of the soldier cannot produce the captain. And Cæsar began his military career at an age when that of the others — except Frederick — had ceased.

A comparison of ages is interesting. Alexander made his marvellous campaigns between twenty-one and thirty-three years of age. Gustavus Adolphus' independent military career was from seventeen to thirty-eight, the last two years being those which entitle him to rank with the great captains. Hannibal began at twenty-six and never left the harness till he was forty-five. Napoleon's wonderful wars began at twenty-seven and ended at forty-six. Frederick opened his Silesian struggles at twenty-nine and closed them at fifty-one; the Seven

73

Years' War ran from his forty-fifth to his fifty-second year. Cæsar began at forty-two and ended at fifty-five. Thus the only two of the great captains whose best work was done near the fifties were Cæsar and Frederick. Of the others, Hannibal and Gustavus Adolphus were most admirable in the thirties, Napoleon between twenty-seven and thirty-nine, Alexander in the twenties. To take the age of each in the middle of his military career, Alexander and Gustavus were twenty-seven, Hannibal thirty-six, Napoleon thirty-seven, Frederick forty, and Cæsar forty-eight. Or, to place each at the height of his ability, Alexander was twenty-five, Hannibal thirty-four, Gustavus thirty-seven, Napoleon thirty-nine, Frederick forty-five, Cæsar fifty-two.

Cæsar's youth had been that of a young man of the upper-tendom, with a not unusual mixture of high breeding and vices, and was rather inclined to be a dandy, — but one of whom Sulla remarked that " it would be well to have an eye to yonder dandy." In manhood he can socially be best described as a thorough man of the world, able and attractive ; in stirring political life always remarkable for what he did and the way in which he did it.

When Cæsar was forty-two he was chosen Consul and received Gaul as his province (B.C. 58). Pompey, Crassus and he divided the power of the Roman state. Cæsar proposed to himself, eventually, to monopolize it. His reasons do not here concern us. For this purpose he needed a thorough knowledge of war and an army devoted to his interests. He had neither, but he made Gaul furnish him both. Let us follow Cæsar in a cursory

way through all his campaigns and see what the grain of
the man does to make the general; for here we have the
remarkable spectacle of a man entering middle life, who,
beginning without military knowledge or experience, by
his own unaided efforts rises to be one of the few great

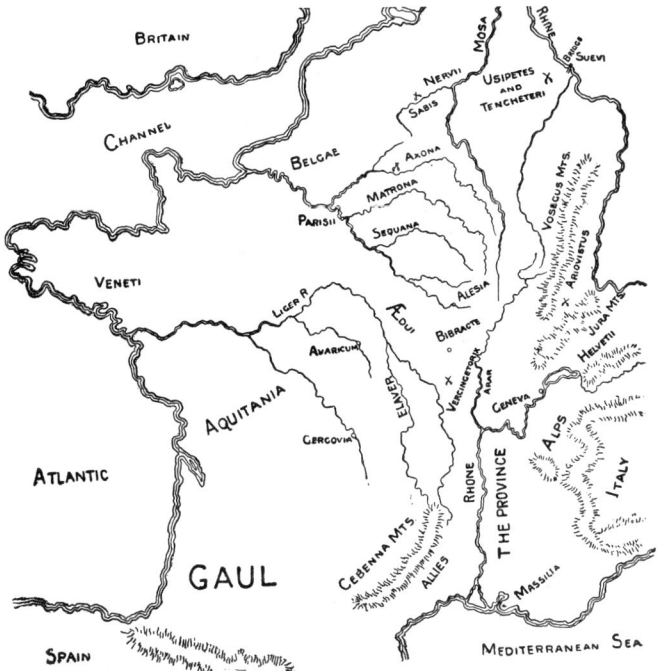

captains. I shall speak more of the Gallic War, because
its grand strategy is not often pointed out.

Cæsar's object in Gaul was not merely to protect Roman
nterests. He needed war to further his schemes of cen-
tralization. On reaching the Province, as was called the
territory at that time held by Rome in Gaul (B.C. 58),
he encountered an armed migration of the Helvetii.

moving from the Alps, by way of Geneva, towards the fertile lowlands. This was a dangerous threat to the Province, and, moreover, to attack this tribe would serve as initiation to Cæsar and his men. He commanded the Helvetii to return to their homes, which being refused, he first outwitted them in negotiations, until he assembled troops, followed, surprised, and attacked them while crossing the Arar, and annihilated a third of their force. Then following them up with a cautious inexperience, but, though making mistakes, with extraordinary foresight and skill, he finally, in the battle of Bibracte, after grave danger and against heroic resistance, utterly worsted them, and obliged the relics of the tribe to obey his mandate. Of the entire body, numbering three hundred and sixty-eight thousand souls, but one hundred and ten thousand lived to return home. Thus began what will always be a blot on Cæsar's fame as a soldier, — his disregard for human life, however brave his enemies, however unnecessary its sacrifice. Alexander, on several occasions, devastated provinces. But in his case the military necessity was less doubtful; and the number of Alexander's victims never rises to the awful sum of Cæsar's, nor was the law of nations as definite in his day as it had become fifty years before the Christian era.

Cæsar next moved against Ariovistus, a German chief who was bringing numbers of his countrymen across the Rhine to seize the lands of the friendly Gauls. Cæsar saw that to conquer Gaul he must eliminate this migratory element from the problem; for the Germans would be pouring in on his flank during any advance he might

make into the heart of the country. Moreover, Cæsar's
actions always sought to forward Cæsar's plans; only as
a second consideration to protect the Roman territory.
To place Cæsar at the head of the Roman state would
best serve the Commonwealth. War he must have, and
anything would serve as *casus belli*. But, though far
from faultless as a statesman, Cæsar grew to be all but
faultless as a soldier, and his present military object,
the conquest of Gaul, he carried out in the most brilliant and methodical manner.

Cæsar ordered Ariovistus to return across the Rhine.
Ariovistus declined. Cæsar moved by forced marches
against him. After a useless conference, Ariovistus,
who was a man of marked native ability, made a handsome manœuvre around Cæsar's flank, which the latter
was not quick enough to check, and deliberately sat
down on his line of communications. Cæsar was thun-
derstruck. He endeavored to lure Ariovistus to battle,
as an outlet to the dilemma, for he was compromised.
But Ariovistus was well satisfied with his position, to
hold which would soon starve the Romans out. Cæsar,
not unwilling to learn from even a barbarian, resorted,
after these failures, to a similar manœuvre around Ariovistus' flank, which he made with consummate skill,
and regained his line of retreat. Then, having learned
that the German soothsayers had presaged defeat, if
Ariovistus should fight before the new moon, he forced
a battle on the Germans, and, after a terrible contest,
defeated them, destroyed substantially the whole tribe,
and drove the few survivors across the Rhine.

Cæsar had shown the decision, activity, courage, and quickness of apprehension which were his birthright. But underlying these was a caution bred of lack of that self-reliance which in after years grew so marked. He made blunders which in later campaigns he would not have made, nor was he opposed to such forces as he later encountered. Ariovistus had no great preponderance over Cæsar's fifty thousand men. One rather admires in this year's campaigns the Helvetii and the Germans for their noble gallantry in facing Roman discipline and so nearly succeeding in their struggle.

Next year (B.C. 57) Cæsar conducted a campaign against the Belgæ, whose joint tribes had raised a force of three hundred and fifty thousand men. By prompt action and concessions he seduced one tribe from the coalition, and by a well-timed diversion into the land of another, weakened the aggressiveness of the latter. He had won a number of Gallic allies. Curiously enough, all his cavalry throughout the war was native, the Roman cavalry being neither numerous nor good. All told, he had some seventy thousand men.

The Belgæ attacked him at the River Axona, but by dexterous management Cæsar held his own, inflicted enormous losses on them, and finally, from lack of rations, they dispersed, thus enabling Cæsar to handle them in detail. Many gave in their submission ; others were reduced by force ; disunited they were weak.

The Nervii, however, surprised Cæsar at the River Sabis, from ambush, and came near to annihilating his army. He had forgotten Hannibal's lesson of Lake Trasymene

Nothing but stubborn courage and admirable discipline — the knowledge, too, that defeat meant massacre — saved the day. Cæsar headed his legionaries with superb personal gallantry, and his narrow escape made him thereafter much more cautious on the march. Out of sixty thousand Nervii, barely five hundred were left when the battle ended. Their fighting had been heroic beyond words. Their defeat and the capture of a number of cities induced many tribes to submit to the inevitable.

The best praise of this splendid campaign is its own success. The energy, rapidity, clear-sightedness, and skill with which Cæsar divided, attacked in detail, and overcame the Belgian tribes with their enormous numbers, is a model for study. But he still committed serious errors, of which the careless march without proper scouting, which led to the surprise by the Nervii, was a notable example. He was not yet master of his art.

During the succeeding winter the Belgæ again banded together, and the Veneti seized some Roman officers seeking corn (B.C. 56). This act Cæsar considered in the light of a revolt, and determined summarily to punish. The Veneti were a maritime people, living in what is now Brittany, whose strongholds could only be reached by sea. Cæsar's attempts to attack them by land proved abortive, but his admiral, with a fleet built for the occasion, worsted the Venetan squadron, and Cæsar, with needless cruelty and distinct bad policy, put the Senate to death and sold the tribe into slavery. Cæsar was personally humane. These acts of extermination are the less pardonable. His lieutenants, meanwhile, had subdued a part of Aquitania. All Gaul, save only the tribes opposite the British coast, had, after a fashion, been reduced. This third year in Gaul redounds to Cæsar's credit for the general scheme; to his lieutenants for the detailed campaigns. The fourth year (B.C. 55) was tarnished by, perhaps, the most gigantic piece of cruelty ever charged to the score of civilized man. Two German tribes, the Usipetes and Tencheteri, had been crowded across the Rhine by the Suevi, the stoutest nation on the eastern bank. These people Cæsar proposed to chase back across the river. He marched against them, and was met by a suit for peace. Cæsar alleges treachery, on their part, in the negotiations, but his own version in the Commentaries does not sustain him. During what the barbarians deemed an armistice, Cæsar, by a rapid and unexpected march, fell upon them, and utterly destroyed the tribes, men, women, and children, whose number himself states at four hundred and thirty thousand souls. A few thousands escaped across the river. So indignant were even many of the citizens of Rome, — his political opponents, to be sure, — that Cato openly proposed to send Cæsar's head to the few survivors in expiation. It is impossible to overlook, in Cæsar's military character, these acts of unnecessary extermination.

Cæsar next made a campaign across the Rhine, for which purpose he built his celebrated bridge. It was a mere reconnoissance in force, of no strategic value or result. And the same must be said of his first expedition to Britain, which shortly followed. This was conducted with so few precautions, and so little knowledge of what he was actually about, that Cæsar was indebted to simple fortune that he ever returned to Gaul.

The second British expedition (B.C. 54), in which he encountered Casivelaunus, was better prepared and more extensive. But though these invasions of Britain and Germany show wonderful enterprise, they were of doubtful wisdom and absolutely no general military utility. Apart from the fact that they were unwarranted by the laws of nations, they were not required for the protection of the Province. "Cæsar observed rather than conquered Britain."

During the succeeding winter Cæsar quartered his troops unwisely far apart, from scarcity of corn, and relying on the supposed subjection of the Gauls. This led to an uprising, the destruction of one legion and the jeopardizing of several others. The error of thus dispersing his forces was, to an extent, offset by Cæsar's prodigious activity and brilliant courage in retrieving his error and succoring his endangered legions.

In the sixth campaign (B.C. 53), Cæsar again crossed the Rhine, with no greater result than added fame, and definitely subdued the tribes along the western borders of this stream. The work of this year was admirable in every way. At its expiration Cæsar, as usual, returned to Rome.

During his absence the chiefs of the Gallic tribes determined to make one more universal uprising, surround the legions, and, cutting Cæsar off from return, to destroy them. The leader of the movement was Vercingetorix, a young chief of exceptional ability, to whose standard

flocked numberless warriors (B.C. 52). Notified of
this danger, Cæsar hurried to the Province. He found
himself in reality cut off from his legions, and without
troops to fight his way through. He must divert the attention of Vercingetorix to enable him to reach his army.
Raising a small force in the Province, he headed an expedition across the Cebenna Mountains, which had never yet
been crossed in winter, into the land of the Arverni, which
he devastated. Vercingetorix, astounded at his daring,
marched to the rescue. No sooner had he arrived than
Cæsar, with a small escort of picked cavalry, started for
his legions, and, by riding night and day, faster than even
news could travel, kept ahead of danger and reached them
safe and sound. He at once opened a winter campaign,
drew together the nearest of his legions and attacked Vercingetorix's allies in his rear, capturing and pillaging town
after town. The whole opening was a splendid piece of
daring skill and brilliantly conceived.

Vercingetorix was by far the most able of Cæsar's opponents in Gaul. He saw that in the open he could not
match the Romans, and began a policy of small war and
defensive manœuvres similar to what Fabius had practised
against Hannibal. This greatly hampered Cæsar's movements by cutting off his supplies. Cæsar took Avaricum;
but the siege of Gergovia, which place he reached by clev-
erly stealing a passage over the Elaver, was not fortunate.
The Gauls ably defended the town, while Vercingetorix
aptly interfered with the Roman work; and by rousing to
insurrection Cæsar's allies, the Ædui, in his rear, he compelled the Romans to raise the siege. This was Cæsar's

sole failure in the Gallic campaigns. He returned to quell the uprising of the Ædui, on whose granaries he relied for corn, and was joined by the rest of the legions.

Shortly after this the pressure of the over-eager barbarians on Vercingetorix forced him to give up his sensible policy of small war. He attacked Cæsar in the open field, in an effort to cut him off from the Province, on which Cæsar, having regained his legions, now proposed to base. As always in such cases, discipline prevailed, and the Gauls suffered defeat; but Vercingetorix managed to withdraw without the usual massacre. Cæsar then sat down before Alesia, a town on holding which the barbarians had placed their last stake. Vercingetorix occupied it with eighty thousand men. Cæsar had fifty thousand legionaries, ten thousand Gallic horse, and perhaps ten thousand allies.

This siege is one of the most wonderful of antiquity. It equals Alexander's siege of Tyre or Demetrius' siege of Rhodes. The works Cæsar erected were marvellous in their extent and intricacy. So strong were his lines that even an army of relief of a quarter of a million men added to the garrison, was unable to break them. Alesia fell. Vercingetorix was surrendered to Cæsar and kept for exhibition in his triumph. Gaul never again rose *en masse*. By alternate generosity and severity, Cæsar completely reduced it to the Roman yoke.

This seventh year was a brilliant exhibition of Cæsar's ability in engineering, strategy, tactics, logistics. His achievements are unsurpassed. He had taught the Gauls that they were not the equals of the Roman legions or nation. Still this courageous people was not subdued. They could see that although Cæsar was able to beat them wherever they met, he was not able to be in all places at once. They determined to essay one more uprising in isolated bodies. But this also failed, and Cæsar's eighth and last year (B.C. 51) snuffed out all opposition.

It was no doubt for the good of Europe that Gaul should be brought under Roman rule. But it is questionable whether, under the law of nations, as then understood, Cæsar had the right to conquer Gaul. His duty was merely to defend the Province. Not so, however, thought Cæsar. All things bent to his ulterior designs. His cardinal motive was self. But accepting his theory, his purpose was clean-cut and carried out with preëminent skill. His errors lie more in his political than military conduct. Strategetically, his course was sound.

The Province, when to Cæsar fell Gaul as one of the triumvirs, was a species of salient thrust forward into the midst of the country. West and north of its boundary, the Rhone, lived allied peoples. From the mountains on the east danger was threatened by a number of restless tribes. The advantages of this salient were by no means lost on Cæsar, nor the central position which it afforded. He utilized it in the same fashion as Napoleon did Switzerland in 1800. His first war, against the Helvetii, was intended to and resulted in protecting the right flank of the salient, an absolute essential to safety in advancing into north or north-west Gaul. From this point, duly secured, northerly, the Rhine, and the Jura and Vosegus mountains protected in a marked degree the right of an advancing army, provided the tribes west of this river were not unfriendly; and it will be noticed that one of Cæsar's early efforts was directed to winning the friendship of these tribes by generous treatment and effective protection against their German enemies. When he could not so accomplish his end he resorted to drastic measures. Cæsar thus advanced his salient along the Mosa as far as the Sabis, and could then debouch from the western watershed of the Mosa down the valleys of the Matrona and Axona with perfect safety. For, besides the friendship of the near-by tribes, he always kept strongly fortified camps among them. The line of the Axona thus furnished him an advanced base from which to operate against the Belgæ, and from their territory, once gained, safely move even so far as Britain, if he but protected his rear and accumulated provisions. Having subdued the Belgæ he could turn to the south-west corner of Gaul, against Aquitania. Cæsar thus exemplified in the fullest degree the advantage in grand strategy of central lines of operation. And his most serious work was devoted to establishing this central salient by alliance or conquest. Once gained, this simplified his operations to isolated campaigns.

There is nothing more noteworthy in all military history than Cæsar's broad conception of the Gallic problem, nor more interesting than his self-education. It is true that a soldier is born, but he has also to be made; and Cæsar made himself more distinctly than the others. He began with his native ability alone. He went to school to Cæsar in the Gallic War. He graduated as one of the six great captains. Cæsar was always numerically weaker than the enemy, but far stronger in every other quality, especially in self-confidence and capacity for work. His legionaries would bear anything, and could do anything. They were very Yankees for ingenuity. Cæsar did not mix Gallic allies with his legions, as Alexander or Hannibal mixed natives with their phalanxes. He employed only native bowmen in addition to his native cavalry. He worked his army well concentrated. If he divided his forces it was but for a short time, soon to concentrate again. But he improved every chance to attack the enemy before he had concentrated. Speed of foot, with Cæsar, stood in place of numbers. His objective was always well chosen, and was either the most important point, or more commonly, the army of the enemy.

It was impossible that during this period of schooling, Cæsar should not make blunders — grave ones ; but all his errors bore fruit, and raised the tone of both consul and legions. One can see, step by step, how success and failure each taught its lesson ; how native ability came to the surface ; how the man impressed his individuality on whatever he did ; and how intelligence led him to apply whatever he learned to his future policy. No praise is too high for the conduct or moral qualities of the army. From Cæsar down, through every grade, military virtue was pronounced. In organization and discipline, ability to do almost any work, endurance of danger and trial, toughness and manhood, it was a model to the rest of Rome. And not only his legionaries, but his auxiliary troops were imbued with the same spirit, — all breathed not only devotion to Cæsar, but reflected his own great qualities.

Cæsar had some worthy opponents. Vercingetorix, Ariovistus, Casivelaunus, were, each in his own way, able leaders. That they were overcome by Cæsar was to be expected. Disciplined troops well led cannot but win against barbarians. The end could not be otherwise. And while the Gallic War does not show Cæsar — as the second Punic War did Hannibal — opposed to the strongest military machine in existence, it did show him opposed to generals and troops quite equal to most of those encountered by Alexander. The Gauls must not be underrated. They were distinctly superior to most uncivilized nations. Some of their operations, and all of their fighting, call for genuine admiration. They contended nobly for their independence. Defeat never permanently discouraged them. Once put down, they again rose in assertion of their liberty, so soon as the strong hand was removed. They were in no sense to be despised, and while Cæsar's army proved superior to them, yet, in their motives and hearty coöperation, they were more commendable than Cæsar pursuing his scheme of conquest.

Anarchy in Rome and his disagreement with Pompey brought about the Civil War; this immediately succeeded the Gallic. Cæsar was ready for it. Pompey practically controlled the whole power of Rome. Cæsar had only his twelve legions. But these were veterans used to victory, and belonged to him body and soul. He could do with them whatever he chose. Cæsar was the embodiment of success, and fresh legions were sure to spring up at his approach. Pompey lived on his past fame; Cæsar, on to-day's. Pompey had made no preparation; Cæsar was armed and equipped. Pompey controlled vast resources, but they were not ready to hand. What Cæsar had was fit. Moreover, Cæsar was shrewd enough to keep the apparent legal right upon his side, as well as constantly to approach Pompey with proposals for peace, which, however, he was no doubt aware Pompey would not accept.

Pompey was a man of ability, but age, as is not uncommon, had sapped his power of decision. He began by a fatal mistake. Instead of meeting Cæsar on his native soil, and fighting there for Rome, he moved to Greece so soon as Cæsar reached his front, and left the latter to supplant him in the political and armed control of Italy.

Cæsar was wont to push for his enemy as objective, and one would expect to see him follow Pompey to Greece, for it is a maxim, and maxims are common sense, first to attack the most dangerous part of your enemy's divided forces. But there were seven Pompeian legions left in Spain, and fearing that these might fall upon his rear, Cæsar concluded to turn first toward the peninsula, relying on Pompey's hebetude to remain inactive where he stood. He knew his man.

It had taken but sixty days for Cæsar to make himself master of all Italy. In six weeks after reaching Spain, by a brilliant series of manœuvres near Ilerda, in which he utilized every mistake Pompey's lieutenants made and without battle, for he wished to be looked on as

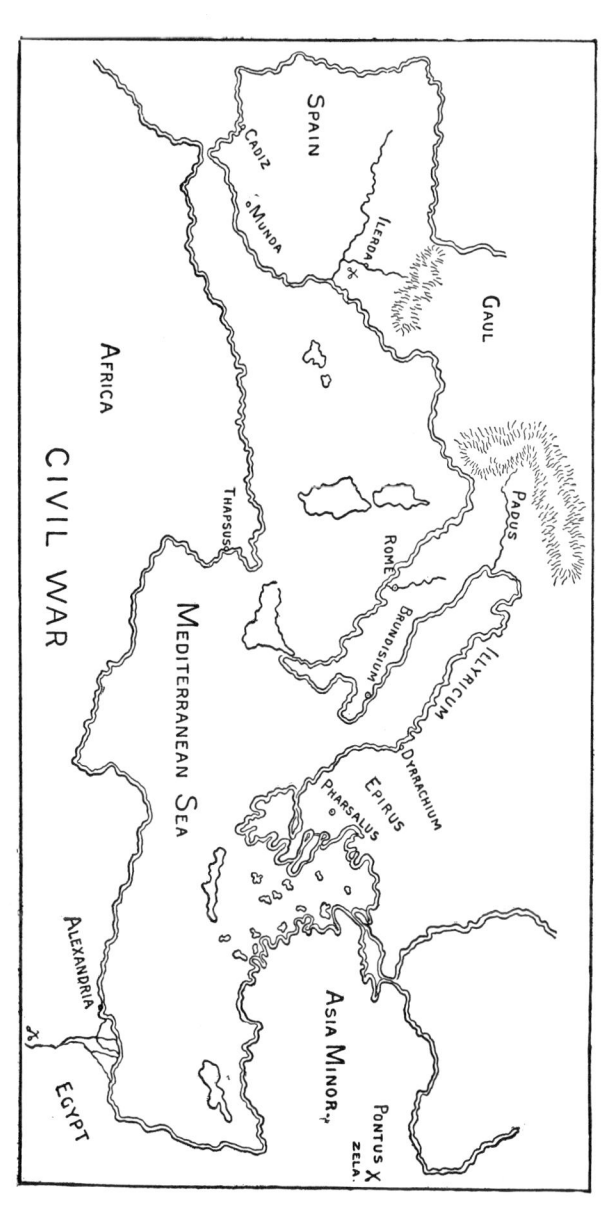

CIVIL WAR

SPAIN

CADIZ

MUNDA

ILERDA

GAUL

AFRICA

THAPSUS

PADUS

ROME

BRUNDISIUM

ILLYRICUM

MEDITERRANEAN SEA

DYRRACHIUM

EPIRUS

PHARSALUS

ALEXANDRIA

ASIA MINOR

PONTUS X
ZELA.

EGYPT

anxious to avoid the spilling of Roman blood, he had neutralized and disbanded the seven legions. This accomplishment of his object by manœuvres instead of fighting is one of the very best examples of its kind in antiquity, and is equal to any of Hannibal's. Meanwhile, Pompey had not lifted a hand against him. This was good luck; but was it not fitting that fortune should attend such foresight, activity, and skill?

Cæsar returned to Italy. He was now ready to follow his enemy across to Epirus. Pompey controlled the sea with his five hundred vessels. Cæsar had no fleet, and, curiously enough, had neglected, in the past few months, to take any steps to create one. And yet he determined to cross from Br undisium to the coast of Greece by sea. It is odd that he did not rather march by land, through Illyricum, thus basing himself on his own province; for a large part of his legions was already on the Padus. But he chose the other means, and when, with half his force, he had stolen across, Pompey's fleet dispersed his returning transports, and so patrolled the seas that he commanded the Adriatic between the two halves of Cæsar's army. This was not clever management. Cæsar was in grave peril, and simply by his own lack of caution. If Pompey concentrated he could crush him by mere weight. But, nothing daunted, Cæsar faced his opponent and for many months skilfully held his own.

Finally, Antonius, with the other half, eluded the Pompeian fleet and reached the coast, where, by an able series of marches, Cæsar made his junction with him. He even now had but about half Pompey's force, but despite this he continued to push his adversary by superior activity and intelligence, and actually cooped him up in siege-lines near Dyrrachium. This extraordinary spectacle of Cæsar bottling up Pompey, who had twice his force (May, 48), by lines of circumvallation sixteen miles long, borders on the ridiculous, and well illustrates his moral superiority. But so bold a proceeding could not last. Combats became frequent, and grew in importance. The first battle of Dyrrachium was won by Cæsar. The second proved disastrous, but still Cæsar held on. The third battle was a decisive defeat for Cæsar, but this great man's control over his troops was such that he withdrew them in good condition and courage, and eluded Pompey's pursuit. In fact, the defeat both shamed and encouraged his legionaries. Cæsar's position and plan had been so eccentric that it was from the beginning doomed to failure. It was one of those cases where his enterprise outran his discretion.

Cæsar now moved inland, to gain elbow-room to manœuvre. Pompey followed, each drawing in his outlying forces. The rival armies finally faced each other at Pharsalus.

Pompey commanded a force sufficient to hold Cæsar at his mercy. So certain were his friends of victory that already they saw their chief at the head of the Roman state, and quarrelled about the honors and spoils. The cry to be led against Cæsar grew among soldiers and courtiers alike.

Pompey believed that Cæsar's troops were not of the

best; that he had few Gallic veterans; that his young
soldiers could not stand adversity; that his own cavalry
was superior to Cæsar's; and that with the preponderance
of numbers there could be no doubt of victory. There
was abundant reason for his belief. But one lame pre-
mise lay in his argument. He forgot that he had Cæsar in
his front. The great weakness in Pompey's army was the
lack of one head, one purpose to control and direct events.

Cæsar, on the other hand, *was* his army. The whole
body was instinct with his purpose. From low to high all
worked on his own method. He controlled its every
mood and act. He was the main-spring and balance-
wheel alike. And he now felt that he could again rely
upon his legions, — perhaps better than before their late
defeat. He proposed to bring Pompey to battle.

The test soon came. In the battle of Pharsalus (Aug.
48) Pompey was, by tactical ability on Cæsar's part and
by the disgraceful conduct of his own cavalry, wholly
defeated; fifteen thousand of his army were killed and
twenty-four thousand captured. Pompey himself fled to
Egypt, where he was murdered. In eighteen months
from taking up arms, Cæsar had made himself master
of the world by defeating the only man who disputed
him this title.

Cæsar now committed one of those foolhardy acts of
which several mar his reputation for wisdom, and from
which only " Cæsar's luck " delivered him. He followed
Pompey to Egypt with but three thousand men, and
attempted to dictate to the Government. In consequence
of this heedless proceeding, he and this handful — he, the

man who disposed of the forces of the whole world — were beleaguered in Alexandria by an Egyptian army for eight months, until he could procure the assistance of allies. He was finally rescued by Mithridates, King of Pergamus, and the Egyptians were defeated at the battle of the Nile.

The months thus wasted by Cæsar's lack of caution gave the Pompeian party a breathing-spell and the opportunity of taking fresh root in Africa. This was what necessitated the two additional campaigns, one in Africa and one in Spain. Had Cæsar, immediately after Pharsalus, turned sharply upon Pompey's adherents; or had he taken four or five legions with him to Alexandria; or had he put aside the question of the rule of Egypt by a temporizing policy, and turned to the more important questions at hand, he would have saved himself vast future trouble.

The force he carried with him was absurdly inadequate. By extreme good luck alone was he able to seize the citadel and arsenal, and the tower on the Pharos, and thus save himself from collapse. " There seems to be nothing remarkable about the campaign," says Napoleon. " Egypt might well have become, but for Cæsar's wonderful good fortune, the very grave of his reputation."

Cæsar was now called against Pharnaces, King of Pontus, who, during the distractions of the Civil War, was seeking to enlarge his territory. It was this five days' campaign (Aug. 47) which led Cæsar to exclaim, " Veni, Vidi, Vici!" And here again he committed the blunder of opening a campaign with too small a force, and came within an ace of failure. Fortune saved Alexander in many acts of rashness; she was called on to rescue Cæsar from many acts of folly.

Cæsar had barely arrived in Rome when his presence was demanded in Africa to put down the coalition of Pompey's lieutenants; and for the fourth time he was guilty of the same imprudence. In his over-ardor to reach the scene, he gave indefinite orders to his fleet, and once more landed on the African coast with but three thousand men in his immediate command, while the enemy had near at hand quadruple the force, and along the coast, within two or three days' march, some fifty thousand men. But again Cæsar's audacity stood in stead of legions, and gradually reënforcements came to hand (Dec. 47). Time fails to follow up this campaign. Full of all that characterizes the great man and greater captain, it not only excites our wonder, but puzzles us by alternate hypercaution and intellectual daring. After a series of movements extending over four months, during which he made constant use of field fortifications, much in our own manner, Cæsar absolutely overthrew the Pompeians (Apr. 46) at Thapsus and dispersed the coalition to the winds. Only the two sons of Pompey in Spain remained in arms.

An interesting fact in the campaigns of Cæsar, which cannot but impress itself on every American soldier, is the handiness of Cæsar's legionaries in the use of pick and shovel. These entrenching tools, quite apart from fortifying the daily camp, seemed to be as important to the soldiers as their weapons or their shields. They often dug themselves into victory.

Cæsar's manœuvring and fighting were equally good. The reason for some of his entrenching in Africa is hard to comprehend. Cæsar was a fighter in his way, but he often appeared disinclined to fight, even when his men were in the very mood to command success. He was so clever at manœuvring that he seemed to desire, for the mere art of the thing, to manœuvre his enemy into a corner before attack. His pausing at the opening of the battle of Thapsus has led to the remark, that while he prepared for the battle, it was his men who won it.

We cannot follow the Spanish campaign, which ended Cæsar's military exploits, and which came to an end in the remarkable battle of Munda (March, 45), of which Cæsar remarked that he had often fought for victory, but here fought for life. We must treat of the man rather than events.

Cæsar had the inborn growth of the great captain. In the Civil War he made fewer errors than in the Gallic. His operations, all things considered, were well-nigh faultless. He first chose Rome, the most important thing, as his objective; and in sixty days, by mere moral ascendant, had got possession of the city. The enemy was on three sides of him, Spain, Africa, Greece, — he occupying the central position, and this he was very quick to see. He turned first on Spain, meanwhile holding Italy against Pompey by a curtain of troops. Spain settled, he moved over to Epirus with a temerity from which arch luck alone could save him, and, victorious here, he turned on Africa. There is no better example in history of the proper use of central lines on a gigantic scale, though the first recognition of these is often ascribed to Napoleon. In these splendid operations Cæsar made repeated errors of precipitancy, — at Dyrrachium, at Alexandria, in Pontus, in Africa. That, despite these errors, he was still victorious in so comparatively short a time he owes to his extraordinary ability, his simply stupendous good fortune, and the weakness of his opponents. In success he was brilliant, in disaster strong and elastic, and he never weakened in *morale*. It is adversity which proves the man.

Cæsar's strategy was broad and far-seeing. His tactics were simple. There are no striking examples in his battles of tactical formations like Epaminondas' oblique order at Leuctra, Alexander's wedge at Arbela, Hannibal's withdrawing salient at Cannæ. Though the military writers of this age exhibit great technical familiarity with tactical formations, Cæsar was uniformly simple in his.

From the beginning Cæsar grew in every department of the art of war. In strategy, tactics, fortification, sieges, logistics, he showed larger ability at the end of his career than at any previous time. To his personality his soldiers owed all they knew and all they were. Remarkable for discipline, *esprit de corps*, adaptiveness, toughness, patience in difficulty, self-denial, endurance and boldness in battle, attachment to and confidence in their general, his legionaries were an equal honor to Cæsar and to Rome, as they were a standing reproach to Roman rottenness in their splendid soldierly qualities. Pompey's men could not compare with them in any sense, and this was because Pompey had made his soldiers and Cæsar had made his.

It is difficult to compare Cæsar with Alexander or Haunibal. To make such comparison leads towards the trivial. A few of their marked resemblances or differences can alone be pointed out and their elemental causes suggested; every one must draw his own conclusions; and the fact that the equipment of all great captains is the same will excuse apparent iteration of military virtues.

In Cæsar we can hardly divorce the ambitious statesman from the soldier. We are apt to lose sight of the soldier proper. The two characters are closely interwoven. In the motive of his labors Cæsar is unlike Alexander or Hannibal. He strove, in Gaul, solely for military power; after Pharsalus he worked with the ample power so gained. Hannibal was never anything but a subordinate of the Carthaginian Senate. He had no political ambition whatever; military success was his sole aim, — and this on patriotic grounds. Alexander was a monarch *ab initio*. His inspiration was the love of conquest, — the greed of territory, if you like, — but as a king.

As a soldier, pure and simple, however, Cæsar is on an equal level, though his campaigns were markedly colored by his political aspirations. Hannibal employed state-craft to further his warlike aims; Cæsar waged war to further his political aims. Alexander had no political aims. His ambition was to conquer; to make Macedon the mistress of the world, as he was master of Macedon, and then to weld his dominions into one body. Rome was already mistress of the world, and Cæsar aimed to make himself master of Rome. Each had his own motive as a keynote.

In personal character, Hannibal stands higher than either. His ambition was purely for Carthage. The man was always merged in the patriot. He himself could acquire no greatness, rank, or power. His service of his country after Zama abundantly demonstrates Hannibal's lofty, self-abnegating public spirit. What we know of Hannibal is derived, mostly, from Roman writers, and these are, of necessity, prejudiced. How could they be otherwise towards a man who for more than half a generation had humiliated their country as she had never been humiliated before? But in reading between the lines you readily discover what manner of soldier and man Hannibal truly was.

In personal attributes there is a divinity which hedges Alexander beyond all others. Despite his passionate outbursts and their often lamentable consequences, a glamour surrounds him unlike any hero of antiquity. But in mind and will, in true martial bearing, all are alike. The conduct of each is equally a pattern to every soldier.

Alexander and Hannibal, from youth up, led a life of simplicity and exercise, and their physique, naturally good, became adapted to their soldier's work. Cæsar led the youth of a man of the world, and was far from strong at birth. He did, however, curb his pleasure to his ambition until he grew easily to bear the fatigue incident to the command of armies. Throughout life he accomplished a fabulous amount of work, mental and physical. His nervous force was unparalleled.

Intelligence and character were alike pronounced in all. But Alexander, perhaps because young, exceeded Cæsar and Hannibal in fire and in unreasoning enthusiasm. Hannibal possessed far more quiet wisdom, power of weighing facts, and valor tempered with discretion. In Cæsar we find an unimpassioned pursuit of his one object with cold, calculating brain-tissue, and all the vigor of body and soul put at the service of his purpose to control the power of the Roman State.

In each, the will and intellect were balanced, as they must be in a great captain. But in Alexander, the will often outran the intelligence ; in Hannibal the intelligence occasionally overruled the ambition to act ; in Cæsar it was now one, now the other bias which took the upper hand. Alexander was always daring, never cautious. Hannibal was always cautious, often daring. Cæsar was over-daring and over-cautious by turns. This is perhaps to an extent due to the ages of each, already given, — twenty-five, thirty-four, fifty-two.

Each possessed breadth, depth, strength, energy, persistent activity throughout his entire career, a conception covering all fields, a brain able to cope with any problem. But in Alexander we find these qualities coupled with the effervescence of imaginative youth ; in Hannibal, with singular sharpness and the judgment of maturity ; in Cæsar, with the cool circumspection of years, not unmixed with a buoyant contempt of difficulty. The parts of each were equally developed by education. By contact with the world, perhaps most in Cæsar, least in Hannibal.

The high intellectuality of each is shown in the art of their plans, in their ability to cope with difficult problems in the cabinet, and work them out in the field ; and with this went daring, caution, zeal, patience, nervous equipoise which never knew demoralization. With each, intelligence and decision grew with the demand. They were never over-taxed. Strain made them the more elastic. Danger lent them the greater valor. With each the brain worked faster and more precisely the graver the test. As good judgment became more essential, the power rightly to judge increased.

All were equally alert, untiring, vigilant, indomitable. But Alexander was sometimes carried beyond the bounds of reason by his defiance of danger. Cæsar's intellectual powers were more pronounced in action than his physical. Hannibal was always, in brain and heart, the true captain ; remembering his own necessity to his cause, but remembering also the necessity to his cause of victory.

All maintained discipline at an equal standard. All fired their soldiers to the utmost pitch in battle, all encouraged them to bear privation in the field, and bore it with them. All equally won their soldiers' hearts. All obtained this control over men by scrupulous care of their army's welfare, courage equal to any test, readiness to participate in the heat and labor of the day, personal magnetism, justice in rewards and punishments, friendliness in personal intercourse, and power of convincing men. In what they said, Alexander and Hannibal spoke plain truths plainly. Cæsar was a finished orator. But Cæsar and Alexander were so placed as readily to win the hearts of their soldiers. That Hannibal did so, and kept the fealty of his motley crowd of many nationalities throughout thirteen long years of disaster, is one of the phenomenal facts of history.

Personal indifference or cruelty can not be charged to

the score of any one of them. Each gave frequent proof
that he possessed abundant human kindness. But Alexander was at times guilty of acts of brutality and injus-
tice. To Hannibal's score can be put nothing of the
kind. Cæsar by no means lacked the gentler virtues.
Some claim for him sweetness equal to his genius. But
he exhibited in the Gallic War a singularly blunted con-
science. Peoples were mere stepping-stones to his progress. Judging Cæsar solely by his Commentaries, there
goes hand in hand with a chivalrous sense a callousness
which is unapproached. He could be liberal in his personal dealings, and unfeeling in his public acts ; magnani-
mous and ruthless.

Alexander and Hannibal were ambitious, but nobly so,
and generous withal. Cæsar's ambition more nearly approached egotism. It was not honor, but power, he
sought. Not that he loved Rome less, but Cæsar more.
He was satisfied with nothing falling short of absolute
control. But Cæsar was not miserly. Gold was only
counted as it could contribute to his success. He was as
lavish in the use of money as he was careless of his
methods of getting it. So far as native generosity was
concerned, Cæsar had, perhaps, as much as either of the
others.

All three were keen in state-craft. But Alexander was
frankly above-board in his dealings. Hannibal kept his
own counsel, making no promises, nor giving his confidence to any. Cæsar was able, but underhanded whenever
it suited his purpose. He could be more cunning in nego-
tiation than even Hannibal, because less scrupulous. He

could exert his powers to bring the wavering or inimical to his side in a most faultless manner.

In accomplishing vast results with meagre means, Alexander apparently did more than either Hannibal or Cæsar in contending with savage or semi-civilized tribes. The difference in numbers between Alexander and the Oriental armies he met was greater, as a rule, than anything Cæsar had to encounter. Yet on one or two occasions, as at the River Axona and at Alesia, Cæsar was faced by overwhelming odds. Hannibal was the only one of the three who contended against forces better armed, better equipped, more intelligent, and ably led. There is no denying him the palm in this. Of all the generals the world has ever seen, Hannibal fought against the greatest odds. Alexander never encountered armies which were such in the sense the Macedonian army was. Cæsar fought both against barbarians and against Romans. Not equal, perhaps, in his contests with the former, to Alexander, he was never taxed with such opponents as was Hannibal. It is difficult to say that either of the three accomplished more with slender means than the other. To reduce them to the level of statistics savors of the absurd.

Each devoted scrupulous care to the welfare of his troops; to feeding, clothing, and arming them; to properly resting them in winter quarters, or after great exertions, and to watching their health.

Fortune, that fickle jade, was splendid Alexander's constant companion from birth till death. She forsook patient Hannibal after Cannæ, and thenceforward persistently frowned upon him. She occasionally left brilliant

Cæsar, — but it was for a bare moment, — she always returned to save him from his follies, and was, on the whole,
marvellously constant to him. Cæsar had to work for his
results harder than Alexander, but in no sense like overtaxed, indomitable Hannibal. Alexander will always
remain essentially the captain of fortune; Hannibal essentially the captain of misfortune; Cæsar holds a middle
place. But had not Fortune on many occasions rushed to
the rescue Cæsar would never have lived to be Cæsar.

In common, these three great men obtained their results
by their organized system of war, that is, war founded on
a sound theory, properly worked out. To-day war has
been reduced to a science which all may study. Alexander
knew no such science, nor Hannibal, nor indeed Cæsar.
What was, even so late as Cæsar's day, known as the art
of war, covered merely the discipline of the troops, camp
and permanent fortifications, sieges according to the then
existing means, and the tactics of drill and battle. What
has come down to this generation, as a science, is a collec-
tion of the deeper lessons of these very men and a few
others, reduced during the past century by able pens to a
form which is comprehensible. Even Napoleon was an-
noyed at Jomini's early publications, lest the world and
his opponents should learn his methods of making war.
We must remember that these captains of ancient times
were great primarily, because they created what Napoleon
calls *methodical* war. It was many centuries before any
one understood the secret of their success. But Gustavus,
Frederick, and Napoleon guessed the secret and wrought
according to it; and they made war in a day when busy

brain-tissue could analyze their great deeds for the benefit of posterity.

Whatever their terms for designating their operations, the great captains of antiquity always had a safe and suitable base; always secured their rear, flanks, and communications; always sought the most important points as objective, generally the enemy himself; and divided their forces only for good reasons, at the proper moment again to bring them together. We find in their history few infractions of the present maxims of war, and only such as a genius is justified in making, because he feels his ability to dictate to circumstances.

War to these men was incessant labor, never leisure. It was only at rare intervals that they stopped even to gather breath; and this done, their work was again resumed with double vigor. Each sought to do that which his enemy least expected, and looked upon no obstacle as too great to be overcome. Each was careful in the matter of logistics, according to the existing conditions. Each was careful to husband his resources, and each had a far-reaching outlook on the future.

Their battle tactics were alike in suiting the means at disposal to the end to be accomplished, and in originating new methods of disturbing the equipoise of the enemy, and thus leading up to his defeat. Each of them used his victories to the utmost advantage. Even Hannibal, though after the first few years he was unable to reap any harvest from his wonderful work, continued his campaign by occasional minor victories, while awaiting recognition from home. Alexander's and Cæsar's victories were uniformly decisive; from the very nature of the case, Hannibal's could not be so.

In field fortification, Cæsar was far in the lead. At a long interval followed Hannibal. Alexander made little or no use of this method of compelling victory. In regular sieges, both Alexander and Cæsar stand much higher than Hannibal, who disliked siege-work, and whose only brilliant example is the siege of Saguntum. Nor can this compare with Tyre or Alesia.

What has Cæsar done for the art of war? Nothing beyond what Alexander and Hannibal had done before him. But it has needed, in the history of war, that ever and anon there should come a master who could point the world to the right path of methodical war from which it is so easy to stray. Nothing shows this better than the fact that, for seventeen centuries succeeding Cæsar, there was no great captain. There were great warriors, — men who did great deeds, who saved Europe " from the civil and religious yoke of the Koran," as Charles Martel did at Tours, or England from the craft of Rome and power of Philip, as Howard, Drake, and Hawkins did in destroying the Invincible Armada, — men who changed the course of the world's events. But these were not great captains, in the sense that they taught us lessons in the art of war. The result of their victories was vast; but from their manner of conducting war we can learn nothing. Cæsar is of another stamp. In every campaign there are many lessons for the student of to-day. In his every soldierly attribute, intellectual and moral, we find something to invite imitation. It is because Cæsar waged war by the use of purely intellectual means, backed up by a character which overshadowed all men he ever met, that he is preëminent. Conquerors and warriors who win important battles even battles decisive of the world's history, are not, of necessity, great in this sense. All that Alexander, or Hannibal, or Cæsar would need in order to accomplish the same results in our day and generation which they accomplished before the Christian era, would be to adapt their work to the present means, material, and conditions. And it is the peculiar qualification of each that he was able, under any and all conditions, to fuse into success the elements as they existed, by the choice from the means at hand of those which were peculiarly suited to the bearings of the time.

Cæsar was tall and spare. His face was mobile and intellectual. He was abstinent in diet, and of sober habit. As a young man he had been athletic and noted as a rider. In the Gallic campaigns he rode a remarkable horse which no one else could mount. He affected the society of women. His social character was often a contrast to his public acts. He was a good friend, a stanch enemy, affable and high-bred. As a writer, he was simple, direct, convincing; as an orator, second to no one but Cicero. No doubt Cæsar's life-work was as essential in the Roman economy as it was admirably rounded. But that he was without reproach, as he certainly was without fear, can scarcely be maintained.

In leaving Cæsar, we leave the last great captain of ancient times, and, perhaps, taking his life-work, — which it has been outside my province to dwell upon, — the greatest, though not the most admirable, man who ever lived.

LECTURE IV.

GUSTAVUS ADOLPHUS.

THE difference between ancient and modern war is marked, but each is consistent with its conditions. In ancient days the armies of the civilized nations were, as a rule, not large. They could generally find sustenance wherever they moved, and were obliged to carry but a few days' victuals with them. Their arms were such as not only to remain long fit for service, but they were capable of repair upon the spot. Neither trains to carry provision and munitions of war were essential, nor were fortified magazines for storing such material indispensable. The communications of an army had not to be so zealously guarded, for it could live and fight even if cut off from its base. On the other hand, battle was of the utmost importance, and the average campaign was but a march toward the enemy, a fight in parallel order and a victory. A battle, owing to the short reach of missiles, was of necessity a more or less hand-to-hand affair. First, the light troops, archers and slingers, advanced like our skirmishers, and opened the fighting. They were then withdrawn and the lines of heavy foot advanced to within javelin-throwing distance. Here they stood and cast their weapons, with

107

which the light troops kept them supplied. At intervals groups from the lines closed and the sword was used, or the heavy thrusting pike. Meanwhile the cavalry, always on the extreme wings, charged the enemy's, and if it could defeat it, wheeled in on the flanks of the infantry, and this was apt to decide the day.

Once engaged, an army could not be withdrawn, as ours can be, under cover of artillery, whose effective use from a distance over the heads of the troops will retard or prevent the enemy's pursuit. Battles joined had to be fought out to the end. Thus victory to one was wont to be annihilation to the other. From these simple conditions it resulted that the art of war among the ancients was confined to tactical values, or the evolutions of the battle-field, and to fortification and sieges. The ancient military writings cover no other ground. There was little conception of what we call strategy, — the art of so moving armies over the surface of a country, that as great damage may be done to the enemy as by battle, or at least that the enemy may be so compromised as that a victory over him shall be a decisive one. Strategy among the ancients was mere stratagem, — except in the case of the great captains, whose genius made them instinctively great strategists, — for strategy is the highest grade of intellectual common sense. But the reasons for their strategic movements were not understood by the rest of the world, as we to-day can understand them. Others could not make sound strategic manœuvres, and saw good in naught but battle.

From the time of Cæsar, there was a gradual decline in the conduct of war, which he had so highly illustrated, and there is little, from his age to the invention of gunpowder, which has any bearing of value on the art to-day. There were great generals, there were victories which changed the destinies of the world, but there was no method in war. For many centuries there was scarcely such a thing as an art of war. One might say that matters had reverted to the old lack of system antedating Alexander.

After the discovery of gunpowder, however, there was a gradual revival of scientific, or more properly methodical war, to which Gustavus Adolphus gave the first intellectual impulse. The conditions of warfare became completely changed by this great invention in ballistics. Fire-arms soon got into the hands of both infantry and cavalry. Artillery took on importance and effectiveness. Armies became numerically stronger, depots for the needful materials were established in their rear, and the troops were supplied from these depots. This gave great importance to fortifying cities and to fortresses, in which lay the provision and war material; and as rations, ammunition, and stores had to be constantly brought from these depots to the front, — to maintain the communications of the armies with these strong places became a matter of primary importance. For the loss of a great fortress containing the army's bread and powder and ball might have as grave consequences as the loss of a battle, — even graver.

Armies, thus handicapped with heavier trains and with artillery-parks, had less mobility, and were less fitted for pursuit than the old troops, which could carry all they needed with them. Victories were not followed up. Battles became less decisive, and dropped into disuse.

Strategy had not yet grown to be the science to which Gustavus Adolphus, Frederick, and Napoleon elevated it, and generals had not learned so to manœuvre as to make battles decisive when won. Modern war, up to the days of Gustavus, was clumsy and lacking in general scheme. It was rescued from this condition by the Swedish king.

In antiquity, battle was the head and front of all things, and armies were nimble and independent. In the seventeenth century, on the contrary, the construction and preservation of fortresses and depots, and communications with these, and operations against the enemy's fortresses, depots, and communications became the chief study. This marked difference in system is shown in the military literature of these periods. Any operations which lay outside of battle, the ancients ascribed to the genius of the general, assumed that these were subject to no method and could not be learned; or at best classed them with mere stratagems. Their object and scope was not understood, nor indeed considered of much moment. Older military literature does not in any sense deal with them. Soldiers believed that the whole success of war was based on courage and hard knocks.

But about the time of the Thirty Years' War, theorists had discovered that there were other means, besides battle, of doing harm to the enemy, and began to reduce such principles as they could extract from the campaigns of the better generals to a permanent form. Their work was, however, only partial and scrappy. The most important document which first saw the light was Frederick the Great's "General Principles" or "Instructions" for his officers. This paper, written before the Seven Years' War and purposely kept in manuscript for a number of years, was finally pirated and published in 1753. It is a noble work. But Frederick's deeds inspired a yet more important one. Serving in the Austrian army as captain of light-horse, was a young Welshman of good education and extraordinary perceptions, — Henry Lloyd. This man's inquiring mind was not satisfied with the half-and-half explanations which the then military books could give him of the wonderful exploits of the great king, whose marvellous manœuvres he had so often followed on scouting duty, and from which the Austrian army so bitterly suffered. He began, with singular critical and analytical equipoise, to study these and seek reasons for their success. He served under Ferdinand of Brunswick in the two last campaigns of the Seven Years' War, and later was Major-general in the Russian army. He spent his old age in Belgium. Among other works he wrote a "Military and Political Memoir," which contains the important part of his labors. It was issued in 1780. The ground-work of our modern science of war is therein laid down. It is the first work except Frederick's in which are exhibited in comprehensible form the true principles of conducting war. It is here first pointed out that intellect and moral forces combined go to make up the great captain. But what Lloyd says is mainly applicable to his own times and conditions, and is not exhaustive. He remarks that the art of war is, like all other art, founded on well-settled rules, to which alterations can only be made in the application. He divides it into two parts, the material, which can be subjected to rules, and another part which one can neither limit nor teach, and which consists in the ability to apply the rules of the first part quickly and correctly under rapidly changing and various circumstances. This is the same distinction which Napoleon draws between what he aptly calls the terrestrial and the divine in the art. The divine part, says he, embraces all that comes from the moral forces of the character and talents, from the power to gauge your adversary, to infuse confidence and spirit into the soldier, who will be strong and victorious, feeble and beaten, according as he thinks he is. The terrestrial part comprises the arms, entrenchments, orders of battle, all which consists in the mere combination or use of everyday matters. It is singular that this analysis of the art of the great soldier is but one hundred years old, that only within three generations has been recognized its divine part.

The man, however, who has crowned with his acumen the written science of war is Jomini, who first became known as a young staff-officer of Marshal Ney's, and died but twenty years ago. Though he rose to the highest rank in the Russian service, his career was as military adviser rather than as commander. His chief value to us lies in his having collated and so plainly set down the lessons taught by the great captains, particularly Frederick and Napoleon, that all may now study them, as during the last century they could not be studied, — were not even understood. He has enabled us to assimilate the history of war.

Other military students have since written with equal profundity. But our debt to Jomini is not lessened thereby. Gustavus Adolphus was born in Stockholm, in 1594, the son of Charles IX. of Sweden, but at a time when his cousin Sigismund III. occupied the throne. He was a lad of great personal beauty and strength, and his naturally bright mind profited well by the careful training he received. His boyhood showed all the traits of strong earnestness, clean-cut courage, and deep religious feeling which later characterized the Champion of the Reformation. Of naturally quick temper, in youth a blow followed a word; in manhood he acquired exceptional self-control. His education was largely under the direction of Oxenstiern, who later became his prime-minister, general, and greatest intimate. He was a constant reader, an eloquent and persuasive speaker, a poet whose religious verses are still sung in every household of Sweden. He was famous in athletics, and was both a noted rider and able swordsman.

The Swedish government was an elective-hereditary monarchy. Sigismund, a bigoted Catholic, was deposed when Gustavus was ten years old, and the lad's father made king. Sigismund retired to Poland, of which country he was also monarch, and remained thereafter the sworn enemy of Charles and of Gustavus.

The young prince went through every step of military rank and training, and at seventeen was declared of age and participated with distinguished credit, and rare skill and enterprise, in a war with Denmark. In this same year (A.D. 1611) his father died, and, against all precedent, Gustavus Adolphus was chosen king. During his reign of twenty-one years, his people and he were an unit. The world has never seen a more striking instance of mutual love and confidence, justly earned, between king and people.

Sweden was at war with Denmark, Russia, and Poland. Gustavus determined to finish each war, if possible, singly and in turn. From the very beginning he showed in his military conduct that his intelligence ranged beyond the conventional method of conducting war, which he had been taught with so much care. In 1613 he conquered a peace with Denmark.

In 1614 he began war with Russia, making, meanwhile, a two years' truce with Poland. In this year, and the next, he drew the attention of all Europe to his bold invasion of the Russian territory, at the point where now stands St. Petersburg, and was for the first time approached by the Protestants of Germany with a request to aid their cause. In 1617 Gustavus conquered a peace with Russia.

Sigismund would not hear of peace, but under the curious habit of that day, of conducting war on a sort of picnic system, he did extend the existing truce for five years. At its expiration, in 1621, active war began. Gustavus, with twenty-four thousand men, making Livonia his objective, landed at Riga, took the place, and from thence as a base, conducted his campaign.

Sigismund represented the Catholic element; Gustavus was the most prominent Protestant prince, and as such received many urgent petitions for help from the harassed Protestants of Germany. The eventual necessity of taking a share in the religious war was clearly foreseen by Sweden. With the advice and consent of the ministry and people, Gustavus reorganized the army and created a distinctly national force of eighty thousand men, and based its discipline and character on the most intelligent foundation. Sweden thus acquired the first modern regular military organization. Other nations, as a rule, whenever a war was imminent, raised troops from the crowds of soldiers of fortune, with whom all Europe swarmed, and discharged them after its expiration. The Swedish organization consisted of one-quarter regular troops for service out of the country, and three-quarters landwehr for the defence of the Fatherland and for filling gaps in the regulars. Recruitment was by districts on a well-settled plan of quotas. The troops in service and the militia were scrupulously drilled and taught, uniformed, well armed and fed, and regularly paid.

The Polish war lasted until 1629, the campaigns being annual, but varying in scope. Gustavus invariably took the offensive, and was habitually successful. He was always head and front of every movement, full of intelligence, activity, and courage, ran constantly great personal danger, and suffered from frequent wounds. No character of modern history exhibits the qualities of the ancient hero so distinctly as Gustavus Adolphus. Cautious and intelligent to a marked degree in his campaigns, he was in battle a very Alexander for audacity and chivalrous bearing. Always in the thickest of the fray, he led his men in person, and, despite the protests of his generals and suite, could never be restrained from exposing himself at the point of greatest importance. He was unwisely reckless of his own safety, though never losing for a moment his cool calculation or power to gauge the situation. His army partook his enthusiasm, as it shared his earnest religious feeling, and was devotedly attached to him as man and king.

In 1628, Wallenstein, the distinguished commander of the Imperial forces, had won great success in northern Germany, and had laid siege to Stralsund. The German Protestants again turned with piteous appeals to Gustavus. The king well knew that sooner or later Protestant Sweden must, in self-defence, enter the lists against the Catholic Empire, and threw a Swedish garrison into Stralsund, which, gallantly backed by the citizens, held the place against Wallenstein's best efforts.

In the campaign of 1629, the Emperor sent an army to reënforce the Poles. This the more impelled Gustavus to actively embrace the Protestant cause. At the end of this campaign, Sigismund, largely under the influence of Richelieu, was prevailed on to agree to a six years' truce. France could not openly join the Protestants in their struggle against the Catholic Emperor, but was glad to see Gustavus do so in order to check such success by Ferdinand as might disturb the balance of power.

This truce ended the Swedish-Polish wars, which had lasted eight years (1621-1629). The king had conducted six campaigns against Poland, and two against Denmark and Russia. These were to him what the Gallic campaigns were to Cæsar, a practical school of war, in which both he could learn his trade, and his army be disciplined and toughened. He had observed the practical working of his new army organization, and learned the weak points of the existing system of war. Comparison showed the advantages of his own conceptions. In the three remaining years of his life he moulded these into a new art, which pointed the way back to a system full of intellectual and moral force as well as more consonant with common Christian charity. The king, during this period, gleaned varied experience. He learned the habits of different leaders and armies, and how to adapt his own ways to theirs. His infantry underwent a good schooling. His cavalry he gradually improved by imitating the admirable Polish horsemen, and by adding discipline and *ensemble* to it. His artillery gave a good account of itself. Under Gustavus' careful eye, every branch of the service during these campaigns grew in efficiency. Equipment, arms, rationing, medical attendance, drill and discipline, field-manœuvres, camp and garrison duty, reached a high grade of perfection. Each year added to the skill and self-poise of the Swedish forces. They were distinctly superior to any European army of the day.

Not only had Gustavus learned to know his generals and men, but these had gauged their king. There had arisen between them that mutual confidence, esteem, and affection which only great souls ever evoke and keep. And as there was no danger or labor of which Gustavus did not bear with them his equal part, so the Swedish army saw in its king a harbinger of victory, a sure protection in disaster. Gustavus' own character, his bravery, religious ardor, honesty, and humanity infused itself into every soldier in the Swedish ranks.

Gustavus Adolphus was now in a position to afford

efficient aid to the German Protestants. The efforts of
the latter had been noble, but far from systematic, and
they were fast being driven to the wall. The war had
been marked by barbarities characteristic of religious
struggles, and by the adoption of happy-go-lucky plans of
campaign. Armies had moved into a province, not because
it was strategically important, but because it was rich in
plunder. Manœuvres were conducted without reference to
base or communications. There was no aim beyond tem-
porary expediency in any one's movements. A fortress
would arrest the march of an army, which would sit down
before it without the remotest conception of whether its
capture would have an effect on the general result. Lack
of system was supplemented by religious fanaticism,
which made everything redolent of atrocity. No general
but was characterized by some fearful vice. Gustavus
Adolphus was destined to change all this in a short two
years.

As a soldier Gustavus is less noted for his battles than
for the conduct, in 1630, 1631, and 1632, of a campaign
on one broad, intelligent, far-seeing plan, from which he
never swerved. This of itself was an entire novelty in
this period of shallow operations. In lieu of detailing
one of his manœuvres, I will give a hasty sketch of his
entire plan of campaign in Germany. This was the first
crisply strategic series of operations since the days of
Cæsar.

It was clear that if the Emperor overcame the Protestants of Germany he would turn on Sweden. To await
attack was the preference of the Swedish ministry. But

Gustavus pointed out the advantages of an immediate offensive war in Germany. The struggle would be kept from Swedish territory. The Emperor would not gain so much headway as to lay Sweden open to an exhausting war. They owed a duty to their oppressed Protestant brethren. He convinced his people and gained their support. He took with him fifteen thousand men. This number he expected to, and did in fact, largely increase in Germany by recruitment and the aid of Protestant allies.

Gustavus landed in Rügen in June, 1630. He added five thousand men of the Stralsund garrison to his army, and took possession of all the islands at the mouths of the Oder. He then captured Stettin and extended his grasp right and left along the coast. He proposed to base himself on the Baltic, as Alexander had done on the Mediterranean. He took and garrisoned many seaboard towns and others lying not far inland. His army, reënforced by German allies and recruitment, soon rose to twenty-five thousand men, and he established a firm footing on the Oder, which river was an excellent line for operations into the heart of Germany. The imperial Field Marshal Conti, who had ten thousand men in his front, was unable to interfere with his operations. Garrisoning Stettin, Gustavus moved into Mecklenburg to encourage its Protestant princes, further secure his base, increase his supplies and forces, and gain active allies. He relied on collecting seventy to eighty thousand men. Count Tilly had been put in supreme command of the Imperial forces, in place of Wallenstein, against whom the Catholic princes had

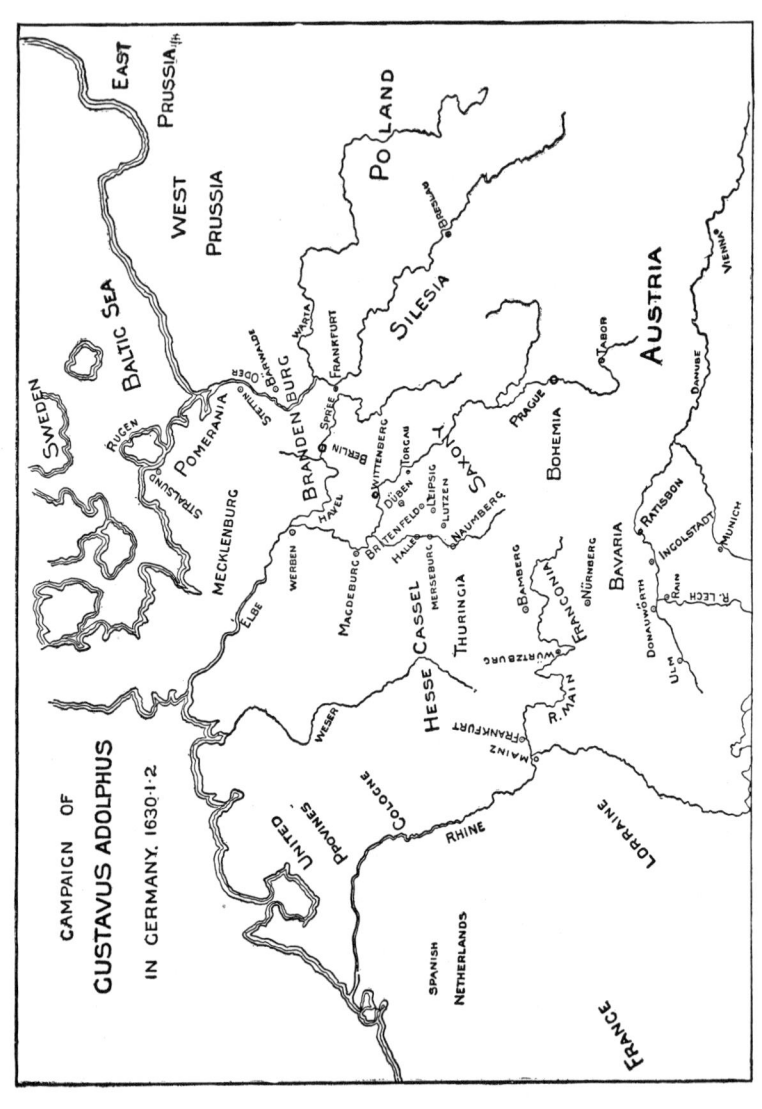

CAMPAIGN OF
GUSTAVUS ADOLPHUS
IN GERMANY. 1630-1-2

EAST PRUSSIA

WEST PRUSSIA

POLAND

SILESIA

BRESLAU

AUSTRIA

VIENNA

BALTIC SEA

SWEDEN

RUGEN

STRALSUND

POMERANIA

STETTIN

BARWALDE

ODER

WARTA

FRANKFURT

BRANDENBURG

SPREE

BERLIN

HAVEL

WITTENBERG

TORGAU

SAXONY

PRAGUE

BOHEMIA

TABOR

DANUBE

RATISBON

INGOLSTADT

MUNICH

MECKLENBURG

ELBE

WERBEN

MAGDEBURG

BREITENFELD

DUBEN

HALLE

LEIPSIG

LUTZEN

MERSEBURG

NAUMBERG

BAMBERG

FRANCONIA

NÜRNBERG

BAVARIA

DONAUWÖRTH

RAIN

R. LECH

ULM

THURINGIA

HESSE CASSEL

WURTZBURG

WESER

MAINZ

FRANKFURT

R. MAIN

COLOGNE

RHINE

LORRAINE

UNITED PROVINCES

SPANISH NETHERLANDS

FRANCE

conceived a marked prejudice. This resulted in disbanding a large part of Wallenstein's soldiers, who considered themselves only in his personal service, and left Ferdinand for the nonce but unimportant armies to oppose to the Swedish advance.

Having substantially rescued Mecklenburg from the Imperialists, Gustavus left a force to operate there and returned to Stettin, purposing to move with the main army up the Oder (Dec., 1630). The end of the year was at hand. The Imperial army in his front was in no condition for a winter campaign, either from habit, discipline, or equipment. For this very reason Gustavus moved against it, his own troops being well clad and equipped, and inured to cold. He soon drove the enemy back to the line of the Warta, and then sat down in an entrenched camp at Bärwalde till he could recruit his army up to a standard equal to larger operations. The Protestant Elector of Brandenburg meanly refused his help to the cause, but Catholic France subsidized the king, and the Protestants called an assembly at Leipsic to agree on new measures of defence.

Tilly now appeared on the scene, thirty-four thousand strong. The king had but twenty-five thousand men and would not risk a battle, neither would Tilly assault the Bärwalde camp. But Gustavus had a better scheme in his head. He planned to draw Tilly into Mecklenburg, and then quickly return and capture the enemy's line on the Warta. He made forced marches into that province, fell on the Imperialists and again defeated them. Tilly, alarmed, followed with twenty-four thousand men. Gustavus, by occupying the direct road, had compelled Tilly to resort to a long circuit. When Tilly was fairly on the way, Gustavus moved rapidly and secretly back to Stettin, advanced on Frankfort, took it after a seventeen days' siege, and thus broke up the enemy's line. The Warta fully protected his left flank in advancing into Germany. Gustavus had completely baffled his adversary. But Tilly took bitter revenge by the capture of Magdeburg, which, though it cannot perhaps be charged to Tilly himself, was given up to sack, and suffered a horrible fate at the hands of his unbridled soldiery. Gustavus had been unable to cross neutral Brandenburg to its assistance.

The barbarous treatment of Magdeburg enraged instead of disheartening the Protestants. Two able allies, Hesse Cassel and Saxony, joined the king's train. And by able manœuvring, restless energy, and clear-headed method he swept Pomerania and Mecklenburg of Imperial troops.

The pusillanimous conduct of the Elector of Brandenburg, under the plea of neutrality, finally constrained Gustavus to dictate terms to him. He marched on Berlin and compelled the Elector to allow free passage to the Swedes over his territory, as well as to refrain from damaging the Protestant cause, if he would not help it.

Thus in one year from his landing in Germany, Gustavus had occupied Pomerania and Mecklenburg, and had neutralized Brandenburg (June, 1631). By holding the lines of the Havel, the Spree, and the Oder, he controlled all the territory to the confines of Poland and Silesia, and with a sufficiency of reënforcements he could safely advance on central Germany.

Tilly invaded Hesse Cassel. Gustavus tried a diversion to lure him away from his new ally. Count Pappenheim opposed him at the Elbe. Gustavus stole a clever march on him, crossed and went into an entrenched camp near Werben. These entrenched camps, it will be perceived, were a feature of this period which Gustavus still affected. They continued in use until he himself in part, and Frederick wholly, demonstrated that entrenchments could be taken by vigorous assault. At this time it was considered the height of foolhardiness to attack entrenchments.

Tilly vacated Hesse Cassel and moved on the Swedish camp. Gustavus had but ten thousand men there; Tilly had twenty-seven thousand; but the king waylaid Tilly's isolated cavalry, handled it roughly, and returned safely to camp. Tilly, despite his excess of force, did not care to risk an assault. Large reënforcements soon reached both armies. Gustavus' diversion had accomplished all he sought. By defending the line of the Elbe and Havel, he prevented Tilly from making any compromising advance.

Tilly was ordered to Saxony. The cruelties here perpetrated by his troops made the Elector all the better ally. He offered Gustavus the support of his army of eighteen thousand men. The king again crossed the Elbe, at Wittenberg, and joined the Saxons at Düben. This gave him a force of forty thousand men, of which twelve thousand were cavalry. Tilly had arrived at Leipsic, and promptly advanced to meet Gustavus with thirty-two thousand under the colors. But, at the battle of Breitenfeld, he suffered a stinging defeat, with the loss of six thousand men.

Tilly's soldiers were in action much what their commander was, — a stiff, dense, unwieldy mass, still hide-bound in the Spanish school, which won its way by mere weight of men in the old phalangial manner. The Swedes were quite a different body. Gustavus had reduced the number of their firing-ranks to three, placed reliance on their individual intelligence, which was marked, and had drilled his musketeers, as well as his gunners, to fire as much more rapidly than the enemy, as Frederick's men with their iron ramrods, or the Prussians of this generation with their needle-guns. In this, his first great battle, the result was, despite the ignominious flight of the Saxons, predetermined by the condition of the respective armies and their leaders. Here, as on all occasions, the king, in personal conduct, was an Alexander in audacity ; a Cæsar in intelligence.

Gustavus Adolphus had been only fourteen months in Germany, but he had by his broad, prescient, cautious, and well-digested scheme, crowned by the victory of Breitenfeld, completely changed the prospects of the Protestants. He had got a firm footing in northern Germany, where he now held most of the strong places. He had secured his communications with Sweden by the possession of the sea. He had grown in strength by his treaties with Hesse Cassel and Saxony, and by accessions of troops from all quarters. He had gained enormously in moral weight, and his army in *aplomb* and confidence. His operations had been slow and cautious, — though rapid when measured by the times, — but they had been sure, and were justified by the event. The late victory had placed him on a totally different footing. The Catholic party no longer looked down on the "Snow-king," as Wallenstein had jeeringly called him.

The Imperial army had lost in spirit and organization that which he had gained. Its present retreat to the Weser opened the heart of the Emperor's possessions to the king's advance. The former's authority had received its first severe blow, and the Protestants of north and west Germany, lately cowed into submission, now rose and joined Gustavus' standard. These fourteen months had shifted the moral superiority from the Catholic to the Protestant cause. But the work was far from ended. It required the same wise and cautious action, coupled with vigor and intelligence, to complete what had been so well begun.

The advisers of Gustavus strongly urged an advance on Austria, believing that such a course would bring Ferdinand to terms. But so far Gustavus' successes had come from a systematic plan of campaign which embraced the whole of Germany in its scope. He had secured each step and had risked nothing unnecessarily. He saw the chances pointed out, but he also saw that if he advanced south, his right rear would be threatened by Tilly, who had, after his defeat, retired toward the Rhenish provinces and there made a new base. The king preferred his own plan of first gaining a firm footing in western Germany. He held interior lines and saw that he could operate against his enemies in detail. To complete his plan would secure him from the lower Elbe to the middle and upper Rhine, and he could then turn against Bavaria and Austria from the west, as his advisers would now have him do from the north, and with distinctly better effect. Meanwhile the Saxons could operate towards Silesia and Bohemia to secure Gustavus' left in his advance, and Hesse Cassel

could hold head against Tilly on Gustavus' right. The
scheme was wise and far-sighted, took into calculation all
the political and military elements of the situation, and was
based on broad, sound judgment. For seventeen hundred
years, no one had looked at war with so large an intelligence.

It may be said that war is a game of risks. But to play
a gambler's game was not Gustavus' *forte*. When the
occasion demanded, he could disregard every danger.
What he has taught us is method, not temerity. His
mission was to abolish the Quixotism of his day.

The Saxon Elector, with a mixed army over twenty
thousand strong, accordingly marched into Bohemia and
Silesia (Oct., 1631) and pushed the Imperialists back
from Prague on Tabor. Everything promised success.
But all at once the Elector appeared to lose heart, arrested
his advance, and opened negotiations with the Emperor,
who, seeing that threats had not succeeded, had tried con-
ciliation. This part of the operation was nullified.

Gustavus moved to Würzburg. Franconia joined the
Protestant cause as Thuringia had already done. Tilly,
having recovered from his late defeat, and his present
position being no threat to Gustavus, marched southerly.
With allies he collected over fifty thousand men and proposed to seek battle. But the Elector of Bavaria, fearful
for his territory, kept Tilly on the defensive.

Gustavus was now firmly established on the Main, and
in Thuringia and Franconia, and he presently moved down
the river to fully secure the Rhineland, leaving a sufficient
force opposite Tilly in Franconia. His men marched

along both banks with the baggage on boats. He crossed the Rhine, took Mainz and transformed it into an allied fortress.

Germany was metamorphosed. The allies had one hundred and fifty thousand men in the field. Recruiting was lively. All Protestants were united in sentiment, purpose, and efforts. France was helpful in keeping the Catholic princes along the Rhine in a condition of neutrality, while Gustavus lay in a central position between the Emperor and these same princes. Bavaria was an uncertain element. The Emperor had a total of but eighty thousand men, and of these the bulk were protecting the Danube instead of carrying desolation into the Protestant territory.

Gustavus now concentrated on the middle Main to the number of forty-five thousand men and marched on Nürnberg, where he was received with enthusiasm. Tilly crossed the Danube and took up a position over against Rain, behind the Lech, with forty thousand effective. From Nürnberg Gustavus marched to Donauwörth, also crossed the Danube and sent out a detachment to take Ulm.

The king was daring at the proper time. His whole campaign so far had been cautious and systematic, neglecting no point in his general scheme. He was now face to face with the army he had driven from northern and western Germany, and was ready for battle. He could not draw Tilly from his entrenched camp; and he determined to impose on him by boldly crossing the river in his front and attacking it, — then simply an unheard-of proceeding. He believed that the moral advantage to be gained by a stroke of audacity would more than compensate for the danger, and danger was to Gustavus an incentive. He erected a battery of seventy-two guns on the left bank of the Lech, opposite Rain, and under cover of its fire set over a portion of the troops in boats, built in two days a bridge and a bridge-head, led over the infantry, and sent the cavalry up stream to ford the river above the enemy's position (April, 1632).

Tilly and the Elector of Bavaria sought too late to interrupt these fearless proceedings. They issued from their camp with a select body of troops and attacked the Swedes, who were backing on the Lech. But the crossfire of the admirably posted Swedish batteries was severe; the Swedish infantry held its own, and the cavalry rode down upon their flank. In this obstinate combat Tilly was mortally wounded. His second in command suffered a like fate. The Imperial troops lost heart and took refuge within their breastworks. Oncoming darkness forestalled pursuit. But Gustavus had gained his object. The Imperial army had lost *morale* and organization, and his own had gained in abundant measure. This is the first instance of forcing the passage of a wide and rapid river in the teeth of the enemy.

The Elector retired to Ratisbon. The Swedes took possession of many towns in Bavaria, including Munich. But the country population was so hostile that a permanent occupation seemed a waste of energy; Gustavus retired to Ingolstadt.

A disturbing element now arose in a curious suspicion of the ulterior motives of Gustavus. Both Protestants and Catholics — Germans alike — began to fear that the king might be tempted by his successes to make himself autocrat of Germany. This feeling soon begot a half-heartedness among the king's supporters. Richelieu feared that Gustavus, instead of Ferdinand, was reaching a point which might make him dangerous to France. The Emperor, meanwhile, went back to Wallenstein, who had been so successful before his deposition from command. Wallenstein made hard terms, but he was a power which could no longer be disregarded. Ferdinand, to gain his aid, gave him uncontrolled authority over the army he should raise and all its operations.

Wallenstein began recruiting. He soon had forty thousand men. The Catholics grew braver when the reconciliation of Wallenstein and the Emperor became known. This, added to the suspicions of the allies, constrained Gustavus to cease his successful offensive for a cautious holding of what he already had.

Wallenstein marched into Bohemia, the Saxons offering no resistance, and took Prague. He then moved to Bavaria and joined the Elector. Seeing that Wallenstein by this manœuvre had gained a position from which he might endanger his communications with northern Germany, Gustavus marched summarily on Nürnberg, which was the "cross-roads" of that section of the country, to head Wallenstein off from Saxony, and ordered his outlying detachments to concentrate there. He had under his immediate command but one-third of Wallenstein's total, and could not assume the offensive. But he would not abandon southern Germany until driven from it. He entrenched a camp near the town. Despite superior numbers, Wallenstein did not attack. He could not rise above the prejudice of the day. He deemed hunger a more efficient ally than assault. He sat down before Nürnberg (July, 1632). The small-war indulged in generally ran in favor of the king, who patiently awaited reënforcements, having provided two months' provisions for his army and the town. Oxenstiern meanwhile collected thirty-eight thousand men and advanced to the aid of his chief. Gustavus marched out to meet him. Wallenstein did not interfere. The king was prepared for battle should he do so. It was a grave military error that Wallenstein took no means to prevent this junction.

Soon after Gustavus had received his reënforcements, he determined to bring Wallenstein to battle, for famine had begun to make inroads in Nürnberg and in both camps. He accordingly marched out and drew up in the enemy's front, but Wallenstein could not be induced to leave his entrenchments (Aug., 1632). Failing in this, the king at last resorted to an assault on the Imperial fortifications. But after a gallant struggle he was driven back with a loss of two thousand men. He has been blamed for this assault. He deserves rather the highest praise for his effort to show the world that gallantry and enterprise are among the best characteristics of war. After him, Frederick proved that good troops can more often take entrenchments than fail. His grenadiers were accustomed to assault works held by two to one of their own number, — and take them, too, under the king's stern eye.

After ten weeks of this futile struggle, and much loss on

both sides, Gustavus, fairly starved out by want of rations and of battle, determined to regain his communications with northern Germany. He left five thousand men in Nürnberg, and marching past Wallenstein's camp unchallenged, moved to Würzburg. He had but twenty-four thousand men left. Wallenstein, who again neglected an admirable chance of falling on Gustavus' flank, soon after marched to Bamberg with the relics of his army, reduced to about the same number (Sept., 1632).

Learning that Wallenstein had left Nürnberg, Gustavus, in the belief that his opponent would seek repose for a period, marched back to the Danube to resume the thread of his own work. The Nürnberg incident had interrupted, not discontinued his general plan. Wallenstein, as he had anticipated, sat quietly in Bamberg. He had shown singular disinclination to come to blows with the king, and exhibited far less activity, though, in truth, Wallenstein was both a distinguished and able soldier.

On other fields the Swedes and allies were generally successful, but finally thirty thousand Imperialists concentrated in Saxony, and Wallenstein joined them and took Leipsic. Gustavus (Sept., 1632) feared for his Saxon alliance, without which he could scarcely maintain himself. He again put off the prosecution of his general scheme, to go where lay the most imminent danger. Oxenstiern again advised a summary march on Vienna, but Gustavus wisely rejected the advice. At that day Vienna had not its importance of 1805. The king left a suitable force in Bavaria (Oct., 1632), marched northward and entrenched a camp at Naumberg. Wallenstein turned to meet him. His evident duty was to concentrate and attack. But, according to the idea of that day, he parcelled out his army in detachments, sending Pappenheim to Halle while he marched to Merseburg. The Imperial general had blundered into a cardinal position in the midst of the allies. The Swedes, twenty-seven thousand strong, were at Naumberg, the Saxons, with eighteen thousand, at Torgau, and ten thousand allies were marching up the left bank of the Elbe. Wallenstein's manifest operation was to fall on each of these forces singly — on Gustavus first, as the strongest. But he appeared to lose both head and heart when facing Gustavus. He grew weaker as Gustavus grew more bold. He made no use of his advantage, even if he comprehended it.

The king had got possession of the crossing of the Saale, but Wallenstein stood between him and the Saxons. Gustavus' generals advised a manœuvre to join these allies, but the king was instinct with mettle, and determined upon action.

The ensuing battle of Lützen has little which is remarkable, beyond the fiery ardor which ended in the death of Gustavus Adolphus. It was a battle in simple parallel order, but the better discipline of the Swedish army and the greater mobility of its organization showed as marked superiority over Wallenstein's masses as the Roman legion, for the same reason, had shown over the Macedonian phalanx eighteen centuries before. The Swedes won the victory, but they lost their king, and Germany its protector and champion.

As is the case with all great captains, Gustavus Adol-

phus gave the impulse to every action while on the theatre
of operations of the Thirty Years' War. For many centuries war had been conducted without that art and purpose which Alexander, Hannibal, and Cæsar so markedly
exhibited. But in the operations of the Swedish king we
again find the hand of the master. We recognize the
same method which has excited our admiration in the
annals of the noted campaigns of antiquity, and from now
on we shall see generals who intelligently carry forward
what Gustavus Adolphus rescued from the oblivion of the
Middle Ages.

The operations of the king, from his appearance in Germany, showed his exceptional genius for war. He had no
military guide, except his study of the deeds of the
ancients, for modern war up to his day had altogether
lacked depth and directness. During the first fourteen
months, he secured his foothold in the northern coast
provinces, in a most clear-witted and orderly manner.
Every circumstance was against him. He had weak
forces to oppose to the Emperor's might. The half-
hearted, fear-ridden Protestants yielded him little aid and
comfort; yet he reached his goal, step by step, seizing and
holding strong places at key points, and accumulating supplies where he could count on their safety. But once,
during his entire German campaign, — at Nürnberg, —
was he out of rations, and this without ravaging the
country. He carefully secured his communications with
the base he had established and with Sweden, and never
manœuvred so as to lose them. He gradually strength-
ened himself with allies and recruits. Unlike the armies

of the day, who behaved as if the populations of the coun-
tries they traversed were of less consequence than the
beasts of the field, Gustavus dealt with them in a spirit of
kindliness and Christian charity which won them over to
his side. He kept his troops under strict discipline, and
by supplying all their wants and paying them regularly,
could rightfully prohibit marauding and plunder. He
understood how to avoid battle with an enemy too strong
to beat, how to lead him astray on the strategic field, how
to manœuvre energetically against an enemy, his equal or
inferior in strength ; how to make the tactical mobility of
his troops and his own ardor on the battle-field tell ; how to
improve victory ; and how to heighten and maintain the
morale of his troops under victory and defeat alike.

When, by his cautious and intelligent plan, the king
stood firmly planted between the sea, the Oder, and the
Elbe, with flanks and rear well guarded, he at once altered
his conduct. He crossed the Elbe and boldly attacked the
enemy, adding to his strength by beating him ; and, leaving the allies to protect his flanks and communications, he
advanced with spirit and energy. In thirty days he had
established himself firmly on the Main ; in little over four
months more he had moved down the Main, and had possessed himself of or neutralized the whole middle Rhine ;
and in twelve weeks thence had crossed the Danube,
beaten the enemy at the Lech, and occupied almost all
Bavaria. Thus in less than nine months (Sept., 1631 to
June, 1632) he had overrun a much larger territory
than he had previously gained in fourteen, and had
added vastly to his standing. He had been bold and de-

cisive, and yet never lacking in the method and caution which were his guide. He had established himself as firmly in southern Germany as previously in northern.

At the height of his reputation and success, he was now ready to attack Austria from the west. But the policy of France changed, his allies became suspicious, and Wallenstein moved toward his rear. The scene changed. Gustavus had no longer the security of whole-hearted allies to connect him with Sweden, and his policy at once shifted to the cautious one he had first shown. The thing for him to consider, if he was to be thrown on his own resources, was first and foremost his communications. With forces inferior to Wallenstein's, he acted on the defensive. With the accessions which made his army equal to Wallenstein's, he again went over to an offensive at that day startling in its audacity. This failing, and provision having given out, he moved, not to Bavaria, but to the Main, to protect his line of retreat, which naturally traversed Hesse Cassel. So soon as Wallenstein retired to Bamberg, Gustavus, leaving a lieutenant to observe him, felt at liberty to take up his old thread in Bavaria. He had gauged his opponent aright. When again Wallenstein, by his Saxon affiliations, threatened, and this time more seriously, the king's allies, and remotely the security of his advanced position, Gustavus again resorted to decisive operations. His march to Saxony and his attack on the enemy at Lützen were equally bold, rapid, and skilful.

Herein is a peculiarly intelligent adaptation of work to existing conditions. From the king's landing to the passage of the Elbe, while securing his base, a cautious, but

by no means indecisive policy ; from crossing the Elbe to
Nürnberg, while moving upon the enemy, a singular quickness and boldness, but by no means lacking in intelligent
and methodical caution ; from Nürnberg to Lützen an
alternation from caution to boldness as circumstances
warranted. After Cæsar's day, Gustavus was the first
who firmly and intelligently carried through a campaign
on one well considered, fully digested, broad, and intelligent plan, and swerved therefrom only momentarily and
partially to meet exigencies which could not be foreseen.
The advice of his most trusted aides was often opposed to
what he did ; but they could not see as far as he saw.
Each variation had its definite object, which attained, the
general plan was at once resumed. There was an entire
freedom from blind subservience to the rules of war as then
laid down ; an intelligent sequence and inter-dependence
of movement on a plan elastic enough to meet unexpected
obstacles ; these produced a perfectly systematic whole, in
which the unity of plan was never disturbed ; and with
this broad scheme went hand in hand a careful execution of
detail upon which depended the success of the whole. His
occupation remained firm ; his victualling was sufficient to
his needs ; his movements accomplished what he sought.

In pursuance of his cautious plan he neglected no essential fortress or city ; he held the passages of important
rivers by erecting bridge-heads or occupying towns ; he
kept upon his line of operations suitable detachments, or
met descents upon it by a prompt movement towards the
enemy. He so managed the division of his forces as not
to endanger his strength nor to lose the ability to concen-

trate. He used his allies for the work they could best perform. He kept the main offensive in his own hands, generally so ordering that his lieutenants should act on the defensive, unless they outnumbered the enemy, and then made them push with vigor. He uniformly did the right thing at the right moment.

The secret of Gustavus' success lay in his breadth of plan, in his constancy to the work cut out, and in his properly adapting boldness or caution to the existing circumstances. As with Alexander, Hannibal, and Cæsar, it was the man himself whose soul illumined his work; and this man had those transcendent qualities which produce incomparable results in war, whenever they coexist with great events. Equal as monarch and soldier, he united in his one person the art of both. His nation and army were devoted to him soul and body. His motives were the highest and purest which have ever inspired a great captain; his pursuit of them was steadfast and noble, open-handed and above-board, prudent and intrepid. In weighing his intelligence, sound judgment, strong will, elevated sentiment, energy and vigilance, he is properly put in the highest rank. But though his record cannot perhaps vie with the others in the brilliancy of his tactics, in the splendor of his victories, in extent of conquest, in immensity of ambition, in the surmounting of all but impossible natural or artificial barriers, in resisting overwhelming disaster with heroic constancy, — still, if we look at the man, upon the results of what he did, at the purposeless and barbarous nature of war as conducted up to his day; if we weigh the influence of his short campaigns upon all

modern war, and consider how his nobility of character
and his life-work has made toward civilization, we cannot
rate Gustavus Adolphus too high. His pointing out the
importance of key-points in holding a country; the value
of feeding an army by careful accumulation of supplies,
instead of by ravaging every territory it enters; the advantage of a carefully drawn plan extending over the entire
theatre of operations; and the propriety of waging war in
a more Christian and civilized spirit, — marks the first step
towards the modern system. Gustavus Adolphus must be
called the father of the modern art of war; and is acknowledged as the one of all others who re-created systematic, intellectual war, and stripped war of its worst horrors.

After his death, his lieutenants tried fruitlessly to carry
on his methods. They retained a part of what he gave
them; in many things they slid back into the old ruts;
and war (except with masters like Turenne, Prince
Eugene, and Marlborough) resumed its character of isolated raids, until Frederick once more elevated it and
stamped upon it a permanence which it cannot now lose.

Among his enemies, during the remainder of the Thirty
Years' War there was nothing but the extremity of barbarous methods, over which it is well to draw a veil.

Gustavus Adolphus was tall, handsome, and strong.
In his later years he grew so heavy that none but well-
bred horses of great bone and endurance could carry him.
But he rode fast and far. His bearing was noble, full of
simple complaisance, and genuine. His quick mind robbed
work of effort; his ideas were clear, and he expressed
them crisply and in happy words; his voice was rich, his

manner convincing. A remarkable memory served to retain the names and merits of his subordinate officers and
numberless worthy men. He maintained stern discipline
in a just and kindly spirit. His religious fervor was as
honest as his courage was high-pitched. The Bible was
his constant companion and guide. He began all his acts
with unaffected prayer, and ended with thanksgiving.
The Christian virtues never resided in a more princely
soul. He was sober, of simple habit, and upright life.
Towering over all around him in mind and heart, and inflexible withal, he was yet modest and ready to weigh the
opinions of others. A tireless worker, he demanded equal
exertion from his officials and aides. But in his intercourse
with all men were kingly condescension and dignity joined.
He was more than monarch, — he was a man.

What has Gustavus Adolphus done for the art of war?
In a tactical sense, many things. Before him, not a few
noted generals had introduced improvements naturally
growing out of the introduction of gunpowder. Gustavus
made various changes towards greater mobility. The
cumbrous armies of the day were marshalled in battalia,
which were huge, dense squares or phalanxes of deep files
of musketeers and pikemen mixed, awkward and unwieldy.
The recruiting of the day assembled many men of many
minds, and the three arms worked at cross-purposes. Gustavus began by reducing the pikemen to one-third the entire
infantry, and later (1631) formed whole regiments of
musketeers alone. He lightened the musket, did away
with the crutch-rest, till then used in firing, introduced
wheel-locks, paper cartridges, and cartridge-boxes. He

taught his men a much quicker manual of arms. The times and motions of loading and firing had been some one hundred and sixty; Gustavus reduced them to ninety-five, which sounds absurdly slow to us to-day. But his men none the less vastly exceeded the enemy in rapidity of fire. He lightened the guns of his artillery, and made the drill of other arms conform to its manœuvres, so that his whole army worked with one purpose. His batteries became active and efficient. In the Thirty Years' War he generally had a preponderance of artillery over the Imperialists.

To secure better fire, Gustavus reduced his musketeers to six ranks, which to fire closed into three. This it was which principally gave it so much greater nimbleness of foot. The troops were well armed and equipped, and uniformed for the first time. Few wagons were allowed per regiment, and effectual discipline prevailed. Severe regulations were enforced. The behavior of the Swedish troops was the marked reverse of that of Wallenstein's and Tilly's forces. Service and seniority alone secured promotion; nepotism was unknown. The force Gustavus created was the first truly national regular army.

So much for discipline and tactics, which, in themselves, are of minor value. But what has given Gustavus Adolphus unfading reputation as a captain is the conduct, for the first time in the Christian era, of a campaign in which the intellectual conception overrides the able, consistent, and at times brilliant execution. From a mere contest of animal courage he had raised war at one step to what it really should be, a contest in which mind and character win, and not brute force. Little wonder that Gustavus, landing at Rügen to attack the colossal power of the German Empire with his 15,000 men, should have excited the laughter of his enemies, and have provoked Wallenstein to exclaim that he would drive him back to his snow-clad kingdom with switches. It appeared like Don Quixote riding at the windmills. But his action was in truth founded on as substantial a calculation as Hannibal's march into Italy, and was crowned with abundant results. The method of his work could not but win. And Gustavus did one thing more. He showed the world that war could be conducted within the bounds of Christian teachings; that arson, murder, rapine, were not necessary concomitants of able or successful war; that there was no call to add to the unavoidable suffering engendered of any armed strife, by inflicting upon innocent populations that which should be borne by the armies alone. In both these things he was first and preëminent, and to him belongs unqualifiedly the credit of proving to the modern world that war is an intellectual art; and the still greater credit of humanizing its conduct.

LECTURE V.

FREDERICK.

WHILE Frederick II., or as Prussians love to call him "Friedrich der Einzige," had been brought up by a military martinet, and had gone through every step by which a Hohenzollern must climb the ladder of army rank, he had, in youth, exhibited so little aptitude for the pipe-clay of war, that few suspected how great his military achievements were to be. But Prince Eugene, then the greatest living soldier, whom young Frederick joined with the Prussian contingent in 1733, is said to have discovered in him that which he pronounced would make him a great general. Frederick had been a keen student of history, and there is nothing which trains the high grade of intellect and the sturdy character which a good leader must possess as birthright, as does the study of the deeds of the great captains, for out of these alone can that knowledge be gleaned, or that inspiration be caught, which constitutes the value of the art. The camp and drill-ground, however essential, teach but the handicraft, not the art, of war.

We all know how Frederick's youth was passed; how his father sought to mould him into the ramrod pattern of a grenadier, and how he avoided the system by constant subterfuge. He was an intelligent, attractive lad, witty and imaginative, and possessed a reserve of character which grew abreast with his father's harshness. As we know, Frederick William's brutality finally culminated in an attempt to punish by death the so-called desertion of his son, to which his own cruelty and insults had impelled him. The succeeding years of retirement were full of active work, and no doubt gave Frederick the business training which in after life made him so wonderful a financier, as well as the opportunity for study; and perhaps the tyranny of his father added to his constancy and self-reliance as well as to his obstinacy, than which no character in history ever exhibited greater. Frederick William, before his death, understood his son's make-up. Frederick ascended the throne in 1740, and from that day on he was every inch a king.

Frederick had certain hereditary claims to Silesia, in the validity of which he placed entire confidence, though no doubt his belief was colored by the desirability of this province as an appanage of the Prussian crown. Maria Theresa was in the meshes of the Pragmatic Sanction imbroglio. Frederick determined to assert his claims. He was, thanks to his father, equipped with an army drilled, disciplined, and supplied as none since Cæsar's day had been, unconquerable if only the divine breath were breathed into it, and a well-lined military chest. Giving Austria short shrift, he marched across the border and in a few weeks inundated Silesia with his troops. From this day until 1763, when it was definitely ceded to him, Frederick's every thought was devoted to holding this province. Nothing could wrest it from his grasp.

His first campaign, however, brought him near discomfiture. Field-Marshal Neipperg quite out-manœuvred Frederick, who, under the tutelage of old Field-Marshal Schwerin, had failed to carry out his own ideas, and cut him off from his supply-camp at Ohlau. Seeking to regain it, the Prussian army ran across the Austrians at Mollwitz (April 10, 1741). Here, but for the discipline of the Prussian infantry, the battle would have been lost, for the Prussians were tactically defeated. But these wonderful troops, drilled to the highest grade of steadiness, had no idea of being beaten. To them rout and disaster on all sides were as nothing. They stood their ground like a stone wall, and their five shots to two of the enemy's finally decided the day. The young king had been hurried off the field by Schwerin when defeat was imminent.

This campaign taught Frederick that in war he must rely only on himself. He never after allowed one of his generals to hamper his movements. Counsel was neither asked nor volunteered. Frederick was distinct head of the Army and State.

In the second campaign the king advanced, with the French and Saxons, in the direction of Vienna. But these allies proved weak, and Frederick was fain to abandon his project. Prince Charles made his way around the king's right flank and threatened his supplies. But Frederick took prompt advantage of this manœuvre, and at the

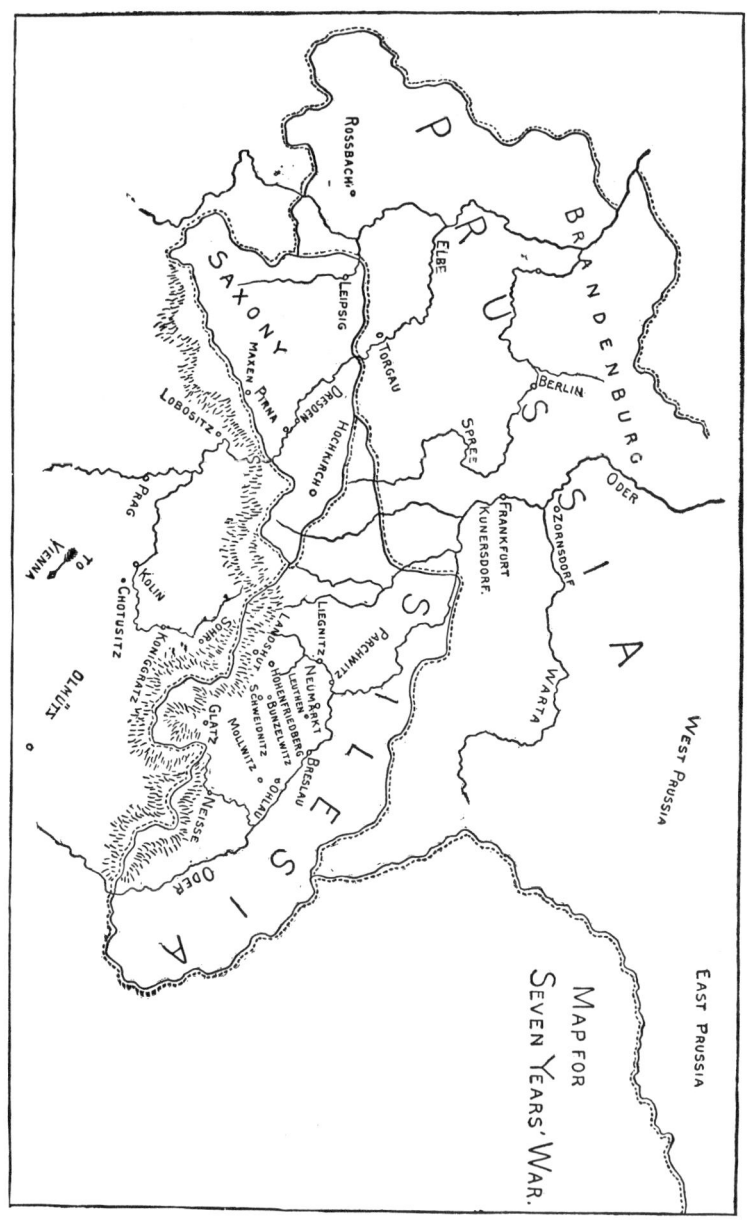

MAP FOR SEVEN YEARS' WAR.

battle of Chotusitz (May 17, 1742) inflicted a stinging defeat on the Austrians. This ended the First Silesian War. Silesia became a Prussian province.

Frederick had learned good lessons. He had gained self-poise, and a knowledge of the hardships of war, the meannesses of courts, and the fact that he could trust no one but himself and his devoted legions. He was disenchanted. War was no longer a glory, but a stern, cold, fact. He had, however, won his point, and he proposed to maintain it, though he must give up the delights of his attractive French Court for the labors of his thoroughly German camp. He had found that his own conceptions of war ranged beyond the stereotyped routine of the Prussian army, though this indeed was not to be underrated. Silesia became valuable to Prussia beyond the wildest dreams of its worth by Austria, and, being allied by religion with North Germany, had every reason to remain satisfied and faithful.

It is generally assumed that great captains are fond of war for war's sake, or for the lust of conquest. While often true, it was not so with Frederick. To none of the great captains was war so heartily distasteful. Not one was so fond of the pursuits of peace. The king had as marked a liking for the pleasures of literature, music, art, the companionship of clever men, and intellectual friction of all kinds, as any monarch who ever reigned. He cordially hated the hardships and mental strain of war. But Frederick would listen to no peace which should not leave him in possession of Silesia. His naturally inflexible nature could entertain no other idea. And for this he would fight if he must.

During the two years' peace which ensued, Frederick prepared for the war which he knew must occur whenever Maria Theresa felt strong enough to attempt to reconquer her lost province. He was abundantly ready for it when it came in 1744. Austria had as allies England, Saxony, Sardinia, and some of the lesser German States. Frederick had France, the Emperor, the Elector Palatine, and Hesse Cassel. As usual, Frederick opened with a sharp offensive. Prague was taken, and from here, the French agreeing to neutralize Prince Charles, who was in the Rhine country, the king undertook a second operation toward Vienna (Sept., 1744). But this was equally unlucky. The French were shiftless. Field-Marshal Traun was joined by Prince Charles, and the two drove Frederick from his purpose. Traun would not come to battle, but worried the king by restless manœuvring. The Prussians were fortunate to reach Silesia without a serious disaster. Frederick had this time learned that confederates were like broken reeds, and that he himself was his own best ally. With the wonderful frankness which characterized him, the king acknowledged the ability of Traun, and the good lessons he had learned from this opponent.

Elate Prince Charles, early next year (1745), invaded Silesia with seventy-five thousand men and descended upon its fertile plains with flying colors, intending to march on Breslau. The king made no attempt to stop his crossing the mountains. " If you want to catch a mouse, leave the

trap open," quoth he, and lay in wait for him, with an
equal force, behind Striegau Water. This time he was
managing his own affairs. Prince Charles camped near
Hohenfriedberg, unsuspicious of his vicinity (June 4).
Silently, all night long, and with such precautions that he
was not discovered, Frederick marched his men across
the stream. His plan was perfectly worked out. Every
man and officer had his orders by heart. Daylight had
no sooner dawned than, with a tactical beauty of precision which reads like the meter of a martial poem, Frederick struck the Saxon left. Blow succeeded blow;
battalion after battalion was hurled upon the enemy with
a rapidity and certainty and momentum which the world
had never yet seen. By eight o'clock — barely break-
fast-time — the Saxons and Austrians were utterly over-
thrown. They had lost nine thousand killed and wounded,
seven thousand prisoners, seventy-six standards, and
sixty-six guns. Frederick's whole performance — his first
— had bordered on the marvellous.

The king followed the Austrians across the mountains.
By careless detachments and small-war his forces fell to
eighteen thousand men. Prince Charles had nearly forty
thousand. Frederick was about to retire to Silesia, when
Prince Charles surprised him, and appearing in rear of
his right flank at Sohr, actually cut him off from his line of
retreat. The prince had bagged his game. But not so
thought Frederick, though his army stood with its back to
the enemy. "They are two to one of us, but we will beat
them yet, meine Kinder! You shall see!" exclaimed the
king, and ordered a change of front of the army by a right

wheel of over one-half circle, under a fire of artillery en-
filading the whole line. Fancy an army doing such a
thing to-day! The manœuvre was completed in perfect
order. Not a man left the ranks unless shot down. The
line came into oblique order opposite the Austrian left.
And no sooner in place than the king flung his squadrons
and regiments up the heights against the Austrians, who
stood curiously watching the strange evolution. So audacious and skilful was the whole affair, and so brilliant the
Prussian fighting, that the king inflicted another telling
defeat, with loss of eight thousand men, twenty-two
guns, and twelve flags, on the Austrian army (Sept. 30).
After some manœuvring, during the winter peace was
made, and Frederick kept Silesia. This was the Second
Silesian War.

Such was Frederick's apprenticeship. He emerged from
it the best tactician the world has ever seen. As a strategist he had yet made no great mark.

The First and Second Silesian wars were succeeded by a
ten years' peace, which Frederick used to the best advantage in military preparations. His army became the one
perfect machine of Europe.

In 1756 came the Seven Years' War. Maria Theresa
had resolved to regain Silesia at any cost. We can barely
glance at the leading events of each year. In 1756
Frederick had Field-Marshal Brown opposed to him. He
took Dresden, and defeating Brown at Lobositz, he captured the Saxon army at Pirna (October). The year's end
saw Saxony under Frederick's control. The campaign
was in every sense deserving its success.

In 1757, France, Russia, and Sweden made common cause with Austria. England was Frederick's one reliance, and aided him with money and an observation-army in Hanover. No less than one hundred millions of population were arrayed against his scant five millions, including Silesia. The allies put four hundred and thirty thousand men on foot, Frederick one hundred and fifty thousand. Always first in the field and retaining the offensive, Frederick advanced on Prague in three large concentric columns, setting the sixth of May for meeting there and beating the Austrians. So accurate were his calculations and their execution by his lieutenants, that in the bloody battle of Prague, on the very day set, he drove Prince Charles and Field-Marshal Brown into the city and sat down before it.

But Field-Marshal Daun was not far off with an army of relief of sixty thousand men. To meet this serious threat, Frederick, from his lines at Prague, could barely detach thirty-four thousand, and in the battle of Kolin (June 18), by a series of *contretemps*, in part due to the king's hasty temper, — though he had attacked and handled Daun so roughly that the latter actually gave the order of retreat, — he was finally beaten and obliged to raise the siege. But Frederick shone in reverse far higher than in success. From not only the field of battle but from the siege-lines of Prague he retired deliberately, without a symptom of flurry, and unopposed.

He was none the less in a desperate strait. He had but seventy thousand men available. In his front were the victorious Austrians, one hundred and ten thousand strong, elate and confident. On his left were approaching one hundred thousand Russians, and these not only threatened Berlin, but an Austrian raiding party actually took the suburbs. On his right, a French and Imperial army of sixty thousand threatened Dresden. The king's case was forlorn. But he utilized to the full his central position. Turning on the French, and marching one hundred and seventy miles in twelve days, — a remarkable performance at that date, — he reached their vicinity at Rossbach, beyond the Saale. Soubise outnumbered Frederick nearly three to one. But in a simply exquisite manœuvre the king took advantage of the enemy's error in trying to cut him off by a wide flank march, fell upon their head of column, and in a bare half-hour disgracefully routed them, with loss of eight thousand men, five generals, and four hundred officers, seventy guns, and numberless flags (Nov. 5). Having performed which feat, he at once turned his face toward Silesia, whence came alarming rumors.

During his absence disaster had piled on disaster. The Duke of Bevern, left in command, had been driven back to Silesia, and the Austrians had captured Breslau and Schweidnitz, and proclaimed Silesia again part of Her Imperial Majesty's dominions. There is something so heroic, so king-like, about Frederick's conduct in the ensuing campaign, which culminated in the battle of Leuthen, that I cannot refrain from enlarging upon it, as typical of the man.

As the king proceeded on his way, the news of what had happened gradually reached his ears. There had been, God wot, enough already to tax Frederick's manliness, and such great misfortunes were fit to overwhelm him. But the king's mettle was indomitable. There was not an instant of pause or hesitation. The greater the pressure, the more elastic his mood and his method. And he had the rare power of making his lieutenants partake of his buoyant courage. Nothing was ever lost to Frederick till he had played his final card. He would rather die with his last grenadier at the foot of the Austrian lines than yield one inch of Silesia. His men marched in light order, leaving the heavy trains behind, and making no stops to bake the usual bread. The king rationed his army on the country. This was not the first instance, but it had been rare, and but partially done, and was a novelty in war. It is curious that so clear-sighted a man as Frederick did not expand the method, so important a factor in speed. But at that day, to sustain an army by foraging in an enemy's country would have been considered an infraction of the laws of nations. The distance from Leipsic, nearly one hundred and eighty miles, was covered in fifteen days. At Parchwitz he met the troops brought from Breslau by Ziethen, some eighteen thousand men. This increased Frederick's force to thirty-two thousand under the colors.

The king determined to attack Prince Charles whenever and wherever he should meet him. He called together his general officers and made them one of those stirring speeches which lead captive the heart of every soldier : " You know, Meine Herrn, our disasters. Schweidnitz and Breslau and a good part of Silesia are gone. The Duke of Bevern is beaten. There would be nothing left but for my boundless trust in you and your courage

Each of you has distinguished himself by some memorable
act. These services I know and remember. The hour is
at hand. I shall have done nothing if I do not keep Silesia. I intend, in spite of all the rules of art, to seek
Prince Charles, who has thrice our strength, and to attack him wherever I find him. It is not numbers I rely
on, but your gallantry and whatever little skill I myself
possess. This risk I must take or everything is lost. We
must beat the enemy, or perish every one of us before his
guns. Tell my determination to your officers, and prepare
the men for the work to be done. I demand of you and them
exact obedience. You are Prussians, and will act as such.
But if any one of you dreads to share my dangers, he may
now have his discharge without a word of reproach." The
king paused. A murmur and the soldier's look of pride
were his answer. "Ah! I knew it," said the king, "not
one of you would desert me. With your help victory is
sure!" After a few more words the king added, "I demand again exact obedience. The cavalry regiment which
does not on the instant, on orders given, dash full plunge
into the enemy, I will unhorse and make a garrison regiment. The infantry battalion which, meet it what may,
pauses but an instant shall lose its colors and sabres, and I
will cut the trimmings from its uniform. And now, good-
night. Soon we shall have beaten the enemy, or we shall
never meet again."

Having learned of the approach of the Prussian
army, Prince Charles, relying on his vast preponderance of forces, left his intrenched camp at Breslau
and marched out to meet the king. He felt certain of

victory, as how could he otherwise? Had not Frederick been beaten at the last encounter and his territory overrun? He imagined that he would stand on the defence along the Katzbach. He little knew this iron-hearted king.

The Austrian van, with the bread bakery, was sent to Neumarkt. In his own advance, Frederick ran across this outpost and bakery and captured it. It was on a Sunday, and furnished the men a holiday dinner. He was glad to learn that the enemy had come out to meet him. Prince Charles, surprised at the Neumarkt incident, lost heart and retired to receive battle in front of Schweidnitz Water. The Austrian army was posted at Leuthen, extending from Nypern to Sägeschütz. The villages in its front were prepared for defence.

The king broke up from Neumarkt long before day. He was advancing by his right, in four columns, on the straight road toward Breslau. Prince Charles lay across his path (Dec. 5). In Frederick's mind was nothing but the firm determination he had expressed to his officers. He proposed to attack the enemy on sight, and under any conditions. In boldness alone for him lay safety, and he never doubted himself or his men.

Riding with the vanguard, as was his wont in an advance, the king ran across a cavalry outpost at Borne. Quickly surrounding it, he captured almost the entire body. The few who escaped carried confused tidings back to Prince Charles, who believed the king's party to be only scouts. From here Frederick rode to the Scheuberg, from whence he could see the Austrian line, and gauge its strength. Careful to occupy this hill and a range of knolls running south from it and parallel with the Austrian line, the king speedily perfected his plan of battle. He was never at a loss. His vanguard he sent beyond Borne

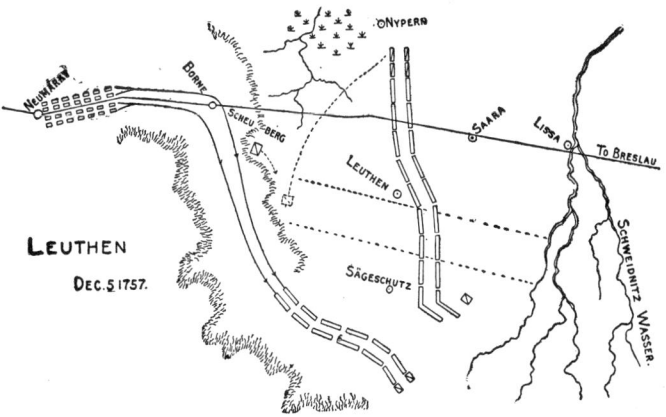

to engage the enemy's attention. He knew the ground well. On the Austrian right it was swampy and unsuited to manœuvring. On their centre and left it was open and firm. The Austrian position, in two lines, had been well chosen, but, almost five miles long, was open to be broken by well-concentrated columns. Nadasti held the left, Lucchesi the right. Frederick filed his entire army off the main road in columns of platoons to the right, behind the swelling hills, and ployed his four columns of advance into two, which would thus become the first and second lines when the column should wheel to the left into line. Upon doing this they were to advance in echelon and obliquely upon the Austrian left flank. On good manœuvring ground and with Prussian troops, the king felt confident that he could strike a formidable blow to the enemy.

Frederick's officers and men had become familiar with this oblique order of attack, from the frequency of its use on the drill-ground and in battle. Its origin was Epaminondas' manœuvre at Leuctra, but the details the king himself had introduced. The cumulative effect of the impact, acquiring power as every additional battalion came into line, was apt to impose strongly upon the enemy. And at the actual point of contact Frederick would have the larger force, though outnumbered three to one.

Prince Charles occupied Leuthen belfry. He could not see beyond the Scheuberg hills. The Prussian cavalry here he assumed to be the Prussian right wing, as it extended some distance south of the main road. The attention of Lucchesi was particularly called to the Prussian van of horse, and he conceived that the Austrian right was to be attacked in overwhelming numbers. He sent for reënforcements. These were denied him by Daun, who was second in command; but the request was repeated so urgently that Daun, finally convinced, moved the bulk of the cavalry and part of the reserve from the Austrian left over to the right, an operation requiring nearly two hours. Here was an unfortunate blunder to begin with. To read aright your enemy's intentions savors of the divine.

The king's columns soon emerged from the shelter of the

Scheuberg hills, opposite the strongly posted Austrian left. To the distant observer they appeared a confused mass, without form or purpose. But the king well knew how certainly, at the proper moment, his perfectly drilled battalions would wheel into line. Eye-witnesses state that the movement was conducted as if on parade; that the heads of columns remained absolutely even, and that the echeloning of the line was done at exact intervals. Each battalion followed the one on its right at a distance of fifty paces. The line was not only oblique from its echeloned character, but was formed at an angle to the Austrian front as well. The Austrian left was thrown back in a crochet. It was the salient of line and crochet which was to be the centre of attack. The manœuvre had lasted two hours. The Austrians had not budged.

It was one P.M. A battery of ten heavy guns was placed opposite the abatis which protected the Austrian left and shortly broke this down. Ziethen headed his cavalry for an attack upon the extreme left of the enemy, to complement that of the main line. Lest his own right should be turned, he reënforced it with some infantry troops. Nadasti had been weakened by the removal of his cavalry, but nothing daunted, he sallied out without waiting for Ziethen's shock, and all but countered the Prussian blow. But though the Prussian horse, charging uphill, for a moment wavered, the infantry on its right was undisturbed. Nadasti was hustled back.

While the cavalry was thus advancing to the assault, the batteries posted by the king to sustain the attack of his infantry delivered an effective fire. Under its cover the

Prussian regiments, despite the abatis which, not quite levelled, still retained them under fire, after a sanguinary struggle, broke the salient at its apex, while Ziethen turned its extreme left. The crochet was thus taken in double reverse, a battery of fourteen guns was captured, and the main line of the enemy was outflanked. It was barely two o'clock, but the left wing of the Austrians had been completely broken.

Prince Charles, alarmed, hurried troops and guns from the centre to the assistance of Nadasti; but the more came up the greater the confusion. Ziethen was taking whole regiments prisoners. Seeing that all efforts to rally the left were useless, and that Nadasti could probably retreat upon the centre while the Prussians were gathering for a second blow, the prince made a desperate effort to form a new line at Leuthen. Lucchesi moved forward by a left wheel. Nadasti fell back as best he might. Prince Charles posted a strong force in Leuthen churchyard as a *point d'appui*.

The Prussian army was now advancing almost north. The new Austrian line lay at right angles to its first position, and, as drawn, encircled the village. The Prussians, within half an hour, attacked them in this new position. A bitter contest ensued around the churchyard and some windmills on the hills beyond. The Austrian line was badly mixed up. In places it was thirty to one hundred men deep, and the Prussian guns cut great furrows through the mass. Still the resistance was so stubborn that Frederick was compelled to put in his last man.

Meanwhile Lucchesi, whose misconception had caused

the defeat of the Austrian left, debouched with his cavalry upon the Prussian left, which was engaging the enemy on the west of Leuthen. This diversion was well intentioned and came near to being fatal. But the Prussian squadrons left by the king on the Scheuberg hills, emerging from their hiding when the Austrians had somewhat passed, fell smartly upon their flank and rear. Lucchesi was killed and his cavalry scattered; the flank of the enemy's new line was thus taken in reverse, and the position soon made untenable. Prince Charles was compelled again to beat a hasty retreat.

A third stand was attempted at Saara, but to no effect. The defeated Austrians poured pell-mell over the bridges spanning Schweidnitz Water. The Prussian cavalry followed them some distance.

In this astonishing victory, which was won in three hours, the Prussian loss was six thousand two hundred killed and wounded out of thirty thousand men. The Austrians, out of over eighty thousand men, lost ten thousand in killed and wounded, and twelve thousand prisoners on the field of battle, fifty-one flags, and one hundred and sixteen guns. Within a fortnight after, nearly twenty thousand more men, left by Prince Charles at Breslau, were taken prisoners.

Prince Charles crossed the mountains and reached Königsgrätz with a force of but thirty-seven thousand men, of whom twenty-two thousand were invalided. So much alone was left of the proud army which was to give the *coup de grace* to doughty Frederick.

By this victory, whose like had not been seen since

Cannæ, and which is, tactically considered, distinctly the most splendid of modern days, Frederick rescued himself from immediate disaster, and earned a winter's leisure in which to prepare for the still desperate difficulties before him. The most threatening matter was the Russian army; the one comfort a subsidy from England. Pitt was clear-sighted in his help to the king.

Frederick is by no means as distinguished a strategist as Napoleon, but he is a more brilliant tactician. He was not a conqueror; he was a king defending his territory. While theoretically on the defensive, he kept the initiative and was always the attacking party. Surrounded as he was by enemies, his strategy was confined to selecting the, for the time, most dangerous opponent and making an uncompromising onslaught upon him. During the Seven Years' War he was placed somewhat as was Napoleon in the campaign around Paris, in 1814, and flew from one margin of his theatre of operations to the other. But Frederick won; Napoleon lost. It was Frederick's fortitude, unmatched save by Hannibal, which carried him through.

In 1758, true to his custom, Frederick took the field before the enemy and surprised him by a march into Moravia and a sudden siege of Olmütz. But Frederick, like Hannibal, was never happy in his sieges. This one was interrupted by Daun from Königsgrätz, and ended in the capture of one of Frederick's convoys by the active partisan chieftain Laudon. Frederick was forced to retire, but he did so deliberately and with all his trains. One of the most remarkable qualities of the king was the dread he inspired, even in defeat. As the Romans avoided Hannibal, so the Austrians never ventured to attack Frederick in disaster. Napoleon by no means rose superior to misfortune in the manner of Frederick. In this instance the enemy attempted no pursuit, and to Daun's utter consternation, instead of retreating on Silesia from whence he had come, Frederick made a forced march around the Austrian flank, captured and established himself in Daun's own fortified camp, and there feasted his men on Daun's supplies. He had absolutely checkmated the Austrian general. This turning of the tables almost provokes a smile. (July.)

From Königsgrätz, however, Frederick was soon called against the Russians, who had advanced as far into Prussian territory as Frankfurt. He marched rapidly northward, met the enemy at Zorndorf, and by a beautiful movement around their position established himself on their communications. Then with his thirty thousand men he boldly assailed the fifty thousand Russians strongly entrenched on Zorndorf heights (August 25). The Russians have always been stubborn fighters, but they now met a man who would not take less than victory. There ensued one of those horrible butcheries which these tenacious troops have so often suffered rather than yield. Frederick won the day, but it was with a loss of ten thousand four hundred killed and wounded out of his thirty thousand men, — more than one-third, — in a few hours, while the Russians lost twenty-one thousand men and one hundred and thirty guns. Frederick, however, from sheer exhaustion, allowed the Russians to retire without pursuit, and singularly enough he neglected to seize the Russian wagon-camp, which was absolutely under his hand. This was an undoubted error; but he had eliminated the most grievous danger from his problem, which was all he had in view.

He was now obliged to hurry back to draw Daun away from Dresden. This he accomplished; but Daun still stood athwart his path to Silesia, which the king must reach to relieve the siege of Neisse. In endeavoring to elude the enemy he ran across him at Hochkirch, and, in one of his not unusual fits of unreasonable obstinacy, sat down in a recklessly bad position within a mile of the Austrian front. Here he remained four days. "The Austrians deserve to be hanged if they do not attack us here," said grim Field-Marshal Keith. "They fear us worse than the gallows," replied the king. But just as Frederick was preparing a new flank march, Daun, who had ninety thousand men, fell upon the Prussian army of less than forty thousand, and, despite the best of fighting, fairly wrested a victory and one hundred guns from the king (Oct. 14). For all which Frederick retired from the field in parade order — merely shifted his ground, as it were — and again camped within four miles of the battle-field. "The marshal has let us out of check; the game is not lost yet," quoth he. From here, within a few days, Frederick made another of his wonderful turning movements, and this time actually seized the road to Silesia. Thus in spite of a defeat and of numbers he had gained his point. The Austrians raised the siege of Neisse at the mere rumor of his approach, and this campaign of marvellous marches left the king in possession of all that for which he had been contending.

But though Frederick had in every sense held his own, and had won battles such as the world had never yet seen, he had none the less lost ground. His three years' hard fighting had robbed him of most of his trusted generals and the flower of his army. He had an inimitable knack of making recruits into soldiers, but these were not his old grenadiers, nor could his dead lieutenants be replaced. The Austrian troops were, on the contrary, distinctly improving. Their ranks contained more veterans, for, in their larger standing army, the losses of the Austrians did not decimate their battalions.

The king's financiering during these years was remarkable. He never ran in debt. He always had money ahead. How he managed to arm, equip, supply, feed, and pay his men on less than eighty-five dollars per man per year, is beyond our comprehension. But he did it, and well too.

As 1759 opened, a cordon of over three hundred and fifty thousand men surrounded Frederick's one hundred and fifty thousand. The king had, however, interior lines and undivided purpose. His difficulty in raising troops — and he had a press-gang in every country of Europe — obliged him to give up fighting for manœuvring, like Hannibal after Cannæ. He could afford battle only when he must wrench the enemy's grip from his very throat. He remained in Silesia watching Daun, who induced the Prussians to advance into Brandenburg, by sending Soltikof some reënforcements under Laudon.

Frederick must parry this thrust at his heart. He marched on the allies and met them at Kunersdorf, and, though he had but half their force, he attacked them with his usual impetuous valor. But the king was over-impetuous that day. Ill luck beset him. His combinations would not work. He tore himself to shreds against the entrenchments and artillery of the enemy. He would have victory. Not until he had lost one-half his army, nineteen thousand out of forty-two thousand men, would he desist from repeated, obstinate assaults. He was the last to leave the field. No such stubborn fighting is elsewhere inscribed on the roll of fame. After the battle the king could assemble but three thousand men. The allies had been too roughly handled to pursue (Aug. 12).

For once despair seized poor Frederick. He thought the end had come. But his elasticity came to the rescue. In three days he was himself again. Every one was certain that Prussia was gone beyond rescue. Happily the allies were lax. Dresden was indeed lost, and Frederick was cut off by Soltikof and the Austrians from Prince Henry, who were on the confines of Saxony. But by a handsome series of manœuvres between him and the prince — as beautiful as any on record — he regained touch and reoccupied all Saxony except Dresden. And although he suffered another grievous blow, and again by his own obstinacy, as at Hochkirch, in the capture of twelve thousand men at Maxen, still Daun made no headway, and the end of the fourth year saw the king where he was at the beginning.

The characteristic of 1760 was a series of wonderful manœuvres. Frederick, from Saxony, had to march to the relief of Breslau, threatened by Laudon. He had thirty thousand men. The enemy barred his passage (August) with ninety thousand, and the Russians were near by with twenty-four thousand more. Despite this fearful odds of four to one, despite the unwonted activity of the enemy, Frederick, by unheard-of feats of marching, the most extraordinary schemes for eluding his adversaries, strategic turns and twists by day and night, the most restless activity and untiring watchfulness, actually made his way to Silesia, beat the Austrian right at Liegnitz and marched into Breslau safe and sound, and with martial music and colors flying. No parallel exhibition of clean grit and nimble-footedness can be found. From Breslau as base, Frederick then turned on Daun in the Glatz region.

The Russians and Austrians now moved on Berlin, and while Frederick followed, Daun marched towards Saxony (October). The king by no means proposed to give up this province. To its fruitful fields he was indebted for too much in breadstuffs and war material for a moment peaceably to yield them up. His stubbornness had grown by misfortune. Knowing full well that failure meant the dismemberment of Prussia, he was ready to sacrifice every man in the ranks and every coin in the treasury, and himself fall in his tracks, rather than yield his point. This wonderful man and soldier was made of stuff which, like steel, gains quality from fire and blows.

The Berlin incident proved more bark than bite, and in the battle of Torgau, though Daun and the Imperialists had over one hundred thousand men to Frederick's forty-four thousand, the king attacked their intrenchments and won a superb victory (Nov. 3).

For 1761, Frederick's forces dropped to ninety-six thousand men. The enemy had the usual number. This, too, was a year of manœuvres, which arc of the greatest interest to the soldier, but need volumes to relate. At the camp of Bunzelwitz, for the first time, Frederick resorted to pure defence. The result of this year left the king where he had been, save the capture of Schweidnitz by General Laudon. Frederick was fighting to keep Silesia, and the close of each year, through good and evil alike, saw him still in possession of the cherished province.

The winter of 1761–2 was one of great bitterness to the king. His health had broken down. On every hand the situation was clearly desperate. No prospect but failure lay before him. He led the life of a dog, as he said. Still the iron-hearted man ceased not for a moment his preparations. He was resolved to die with honor if he could not win. Had the outlook been promising in the extreme, he could not have labored more consistently, even if more cheerfully. " All our wars should be short and sharp," says he ; " a long war is bad for our discipline and would exhaust our population and resources." The theory of the strategy as well as the battle evolutions of the king was the saving of time by skill and rapidity.

The death of the Czarina and accession of Peter III. gave Frederick a breathing-spell. This lasted but a short while, when the death of Peter again changed the current. But the war from now on languished, and there finally came about a peace on the "as-you-were" principle. Frederick kept Silesia (1763).

Frederick had not been a strong boy, but in early manhood he had gained in physique. His life with troops had lent him a robustness of constitution equal to any drain or strain, and his wonderful determination drove him to ceaseless activity. Later in life he was troubled with gout. Even when seventy-three years old, and clinging to life by a mere thread, he never ceased daily, hourly work. His efforts were all for the good of Prussia, and his subjects recognized what he had done for the fatherland. Zimmermann, the Hanoverian physician, thus describes him in his old age : —

"He is not of tall stature, and seems bent under his load of laurels and his many years of struggle. His blue coat, much worn like his body, long boots to above the knees, and a white snuff-besprinkled vest, gave him a peculiar aspect. But the fire of his eyes showed that Frederick's soul had not grown old. Though his bearing was that of an invalid, yet one must conclude from the quickness of his movements and the bold decisiveness of his look, that he could yet fight like a youth. Set up his unimportant figure among a million of men, and every one would recognize in him the king, so much sublimity and constancy resided in this unusual man ! "

And the same writer says of his palace : —

" At Sans Souci there reigned such quiet that one might notice every breath. My first visit to this lonely spot was of an evening in the late fall. I was indeed surprised when I saw before me a small mansion, and learned that in it lived the hero who had already shaken the world with his name. I went around the entire house, approached the windows, saw light in them, but found no sentry before the doors, nor met a man to ask me who I was or what I craved. Then first I understood the greatness of Frederick. He needs for his protection not armed minions or firearms. He knows that the love and respect of the people keep watch at the doors of his modest abode."

Frederick's military genius was coupled with absolute control of his country's resources. Though Gustavus Adolphus was both general and king, he was not an autocrat. The constitution of Sweden prescribed his bounds. In ancient days, only Alexander stood in the position of Frederick, and Cæsar, during the latter portion of his campaigns. Hannibal was always limited in his authority. Alexander, working in a far larger sphere, had personal ambitions and a scope which Frederick lacked, yet each worked for the good of his country. Frederick was not a conqueror. He fought to defend his possessions. His military education was narrow; his favorite studies and occupations essentially peaceful. But from history he had sucked the ambition to make more powerful the country which owed him allegiance, and he had digested the deeds of the great commanders as only a great soldier can. Unconscious of his own ability, necessity soon forced him to show what he was worth. Like the Romans, he laid down one rule : Never wait for your opponent's attack. If you are on the defensive, let this be still of an offensive char-

acter in both campaigns and battles. This rule he followed
through life.

Frederick most resembled Hannibal. He possessed
Hannibal's virtue, — the secret of keeping a secret. He
never divulged his plans. From the start he was a captain, and so he remained to the end. How did he learn
his trade? Alexander and Hannibal learned theirs under
Philip and Hamilcar in Greece and Spain. Cæsar taught
himself in Gaul; Gustavus Adolphus, in Denmark, Russia,
and Poland. But Frederick had had no opportunities,
except to learn the pipe-clay half of the art of war. His
five years' retirement after his court-martial must have
done for him more than any one ever knew. The fertility
of his intelligence, and his power of applying what he
learned, were the foundation of his skill. His first campaign advanced him more than a life of war does the
greatest among others. The First Silesian War was a
school out of which Frederick emerged the soldier he
always remained.

That Frederick was not a warrior for the sake of conquest was well shown in his moderation after the First
Silesian War. He demanded only his rights, as he understood them. And after the Second Silesian, and the Seven
Years' War, he asked no more than he got at the peace of
Dresden, when he might have made far greater claims.
Indeed, Frederick's whole life showed his preference for
the arts of peace. After the glamour of the first step
had vanished, war was but his duty to Prussia.

Frederick had assimilated the theory of war from the
history of great men; but its study was never a favorite

pursuit. He was a born soldier. As Cæsar taught himself from ambition, so Frederick taught himself from necessity. What he did had not a theoretical but an essentially practical flavor. He rose to the highest intellectual and characteristic plane of the art, not by imitation of others, but by native vigor. Frederick had by heart the lesson of Leuctra and Mantinœa, but it required genius to apply the oblique order as he did it at Leuthen. No man has ever so perfectly done this. No one in modern times has had such troops.

Frederick placed war among the liberal arts. Perhaps the least straight-laced of any captain, he held that only broad principles can govern it; that the use of the maxims of war depends on the personality of the soldier and the demands of the moment. His "Instructions" to his generals set out Frederick's whole art. It is full of simple, common sense, apt rules, practical to the last degree. But it was the man who made them so fruitful. Just because they do represent the man they are interesting in this connection.

Frederick is the first writer on the military art who goes to the root of the matter. He always wrote profusely, — most plentifully in bad French verse, — but his "Instructions" are admirable throughout. At the head of the paper stands this motto: "Always move into the field sooner than the enemy;" and this was his course in campaign and battle alike. He asked of the enemy a categorical *yes* or *no* to his ultimatum, and upon *no* struck an instant blow. So novel was Frederick's quick decisiveness that he was at first looked upon in Europe as a rank dis-

turber of the peace. But his was only the old Roman
method revamped.

Underlying this rule was the good of Prussia. This
motive he ground into his men's souls. He demanded as
a daily habit extraordinary exertions. His men must perform the unusual at all times. And "from highest officer
to last private, no one is to argue, but to obey," says he.
A habit of obedience supplanted fear of punishment. The
king's zeal flowed down through every channel to the
ranks. He was himself notoriously the hardest-worked
man in Prussia, and his men appreciated the fact.

Next in importance to discipline comes the care of the
troops. In his day subsistence tied armies down to predetermined manœuvres. Frederick carried his rations with
him, and in his rapid movements made requisitions on the
country, as Napoleon, a generation later, did more fully.

Then follows the study of topography. Positions were
to Frederick only links in a chain, or resting places, but he
ably utilized the lay of the land in his battles. He taught
his generals, wherever they might be, to look at the surrounding country and ask themselves, "What should I do
if I was suddenly attacked in this position?" He enunciated many maxims scarcely known at his day. "If you
divide your forces you will be beaten in detail. If you
wish to deliver a battle bring together as many troops as
possible." Frederick did not try to keep everything, but
put all his energy into the one important matter. His was
no hard and fast system. He did what was most apt.
His battle plans were conceived instantly on the ground.
What was intricate to others was simple to him and to the

Prussian army. Frederick held Hannibal up as a pattern. "Always," said the king, "lead the enemy to believe you will do the very reverse of what you intend to do." Minor operations are clearly treated of. In general the *motif* of these "Instructions" is attack and initiative. " Prussians," said he, "are invariably to attack the enemy." Close with him even if weaker. Make up for weakness by boldness and energy. He opposed passive defence. Every one of his battles was offensive. He complained, indeed, that he had to risk much all his life.

Frederick's irrepressible courage under misfortune is equalled in history only by Hannibal's. Fortune was not his servant as she was Alexander's and Cæsar's. He thanked himself for his good luck, or rather his successes were due to the fact that he made use of good luck when he had it, and threw no chances away. The magnificence of his warlike deeds is traceable almost solely to his own mental power and remarkable persistency. No danger or difficulty ever, in the remotest degree, changed his purpose or affected his reasoning power. It was this kept the ascendant on his side.

Despite sternest discipline, Frederick was familiar with his men, who knew him as Vater Fritz, and bandied rough jokes with him. "The Austrians are three to one of us, and stoutly entrenched," said the king, riding the outposts before Leuthen. "And were the devil in front and all around them, we'll hustle them out, only thou lead us on !" answered a brawny grenadier. "Good-night, Fritz." He gained such personal love from his men that it seems to have been transmitted as a heritage of the Hohenzollerns.

He spurred his men to the most heroic efforts, the most extraordinary feats of daring and endurance. As the complement to this quality, he infused in his enemies a dread of his presence. He utilized the mistakes they made and led them into still others, less from any system than by doing the right thing at the right moment. Strict rules aid only the minds whose conceptions are not clear, and whose execution lacks promptness. Rules were as nothing to Frederick. He observed them, not because they were rules, but because they were grounded on truths which his own mind grasped without them. He broke them when there was distinct gain in so doing. His operations against six armies surrounding him was based on his own maxim, that " Whoso attempts to defend everything runs danger of losing everything," and he turned from one to the other, risking much to gain much. This idea of Frederick's was a novel one in his century, whose warfare consisted in an attempt to protect and hold everything by fortresses and partial detachments. In working out this idea he is unapproached.

Frederick never allowed his enemies to carry out their own plans. His movements imposed limitations upon them. He impressed his own personality on every campaign. To carry his victuals with him enabled him to outmanœuvre them, for his enemies relied exclusively on magazines established beforehand. He could select his routes according to the exigencies of the moment, while they must keep within reach of their depots.

Tactically, Frederick stands highest of all soldiers. Strategically he was less great. In strategic movements,

his brother, Prince Henry, did occasional work worthy to
be placed beside the king's. Tactically, no one could approach him. His method of handling the three arms was
perfect.

Gustavus Adolphus had given new impulse to systematic,
intelligent war. But what he did was not understood.
His imitators jumbled the old and new systems. They
placed too much reliance on fortresses and magazines, and
on natural and artificial obstacles; they made strained
efforts to threaten the enemy's communications; they manœuvred for the mere sake of doing something and apart
from any general plan; they avoided decisive movements
and battles.

Frederick, by making his armies less dependent on
magazines, acquired a freer, bolder, and more rapid style.
The allies aimed to parcel out Prussia. Frederick met
them with decision. Surrounded on all sides by overwhelming numbers, he was compelled to defend himself by
hard knocks. And his individual equipment as well as the
discipline of his army enabled him to do this with unequalled brilliancy. In all history there is no such series
of tactical feats as Frederick's.

Each captain must be weighed by the conditions under
which he worked. We cannot try Alexander by the
standard of Napoleon. While Napoleon's battle tactics
have something stupendous in their magnificence, Frederick's battles, in view of numbers and difficulties, are
distinctly finer. Frederick's decisiveness aroused fresh
interest in battle. Manœuvres now sought battle as an
object, while sieges became fewer and of small moment.

All Europe was agog at Frederick's successes, but no one understood them. Lloyd alone saw below the surface. As Gustavus had been misinterpreted, so now Frederick. Some imitated his minutiæ down to the pig-tails of his grenadiers. Some saw the cure-all of war in operations against the enemy's flanks and rear. Some saw in detachments, some in concentration, the trick of the king. Only Lloyd recognized that it all lay in the magnificent personality of the king himself, that there was no secret, no set rule, no legerdemain, but that here again was one of the world's great captains. The imitators of Frederick caught but the letter. The spirit they could not catch. Until two generations more had passed, and Lloyd and Jomini had put in printed form what Frederick and Napoleon did, the world could not guess the riddle.

His own fortresses were of importance to Frederick because his enemy respected them. But he paid small heed to the enemy's. He could strike him so much harder by battle, that he never frittered away his time on sieges, except as a means to an end. The allies clung to their fortified positions. Frederick despised them, and showed the world that his gallant Prussians could take them by assault.

This period, then, is distinguished for the revival of battles, and of operations looking towards battle. Of these Frederick was the author. Battles in the Seven Years' War were not haphazard. Each had its purpose. Pursuit had, however, not yet been made effective so to glean the utmost from victory. No single battle in this period had remarkable results. Frederick's battles were generally fought to prevent some particular enemy from penetrating too far into the dominions of Prussia. In this they were uniformly successful. But in the sense of Napoleon's battles they were not decisive. The superior decisiveness of Napoleon's lay in the strategic conditions and in his superiority of forces. No battles — as battles —could be more thoroughly fought out than Frederick's; no victories more brilliant.

Frederick not only showed Europe what speed and decision can do in war, but he made many minor improvements in drill, discipline, and battle-tactics. He introduced horse-artillery. His giving scope to such men as Seydlitz and Ziethen made the Prussian cavalry a model for all time. He demonstrated that armies can march and operate continuously, with little rest, and without regard to seasons. Light troops grew in efficiency. War put on an aspect of energetic purpose, but without the ruthless barbarity of the Thirty Years' War.

No doubt Napoleon, at his best, was the greater soldier. But Napoleon had Frederick's example before him, as well as the lessons of all other great captains by heart. Napoleon's motive was aggressive; Frederick's, pure defence. Hence partly the larger method. But Frederick in trial or disaster was unspeakably greater than Napoleon, both as soldier and man.

In the forty-six years of his reign Frederick added sixty per cent. to the Prussian dominion, doubled its population, put seventy million thalers in its treasury, and created two hundred thousand of the best troops in existence. Prussia had been a small state, which the powers of Europe united to parcel out. He left it a great state, which all Europe respected, and planted in it the seed which has raised its kings to be emperors of Germany. This result is in marked contrast to what Napoleon's wars did for France.

Whoever, under the sumptuous dome of the Invalides, has gazed down upon the splendid sarcophagus of Napoleon, and has stepped within the dim and narrow vault of the plain old garrison church at Potsdam, where stand the simple metal coffins of Frederick the Great and of his father, must have felt that in the latter shrine, rather than the other, he has stood in the presence of the ashes of a king.

Whatever may be said of Frederick's personal method of government, or of the true Hohenzollern theory that Prussia belonged to him as an heritage to make or to mar as he saw fit, it cannot be denied that he was true to the spirit of his own verses, penned in the days of his direst distress : —

"Pour moi, menacé du naufrage,
Je dois, en affrontant l'orage,
Penser, vivre et mourir en Roi."

LECTURE VI.

NAPOLEON.

THE career of Napoleon Bonaparte is so near to our own times and so commonly familiar, that it is not essential to describe any of those operations which were, within the memory of some men yet living, the wonder and dread of Europe. In certain respects Napoleon was the greatest of all soldiers. He had, to be sure, the history of other great captains to profit by; he had not to invent; he had only to improve. But he did for the military art what constitutes the greatest advance in any art, he reduced it to its most simple, most perfect form; and his and Frederick's campaigns furnished the final material from which Jomini and his followers could elucidate the science; for it has taken more than two thousand years of the written history of war to produce a written science of war.

I shall not touch upon Napoleon's life as statesman or lawgiver, nor on his services in carrying forward the results of the Revolution toward its legitimate consequence, — the equality of all men before the law. In these rôles no more useful man appears in the history of modern times. I shall look at him simply as a soldier.

178

Napoleon's career is a notable example of the necessity of coexistent intellect, character, and opportunity to produce the greatest success in war. His strength distinctly rose through half his career, and as distinctly fell during the other half. His intellectual power never changed. The plan of the Waterloo campaign was as brilliant as any which he ever conceived. His opportunity here was equal to that of 1796. But his execution was marred by weakening physique, upon which followed a decline of that decisiveness which is so indispensable to the great captain. It will, perhaps, be interesting to trace certain resemblances between the opening of his first independent campaign in 1796, and his last one in 1815, to show how force of character won him the first and the lack of it lost him the last; and to connect the two campaigns by a thread of the intervening years of growth till 1808, and of decline from that time on.

When Napoleon was appointed to the command of the Army of Italy he had for the moment a serious problem. In this army were able and more experienced officers of mature powers and full of manly strength, who looked on this all but unknown, twenty-seven years old, small, pale, untried commander-in-chief, decidedly askance. But Napoleon was not long in impressing his absolute superiority upon them all. They soon recognized the master-hand.

The army lay strung out along the coast from Loano to Savona, in a worse than bad position. The English fleet held the sea in its rear, and could make descents on any part of this long and ill-held line. Its communications lay in prolongation of the left flank, over a single bad road,

subject not only to interruption by the English, but the
enemy, by forcing the Col di Tenda, could absolutely cut
it off from France. The troops were in woful condition.
They had neither clothing nor rations. They were literally
" heroes in rags." On the further side of the Maritime
Alps lay the Austrian general, Beaulieu, commanding a
superior army equally strung out from Mount Blanc to

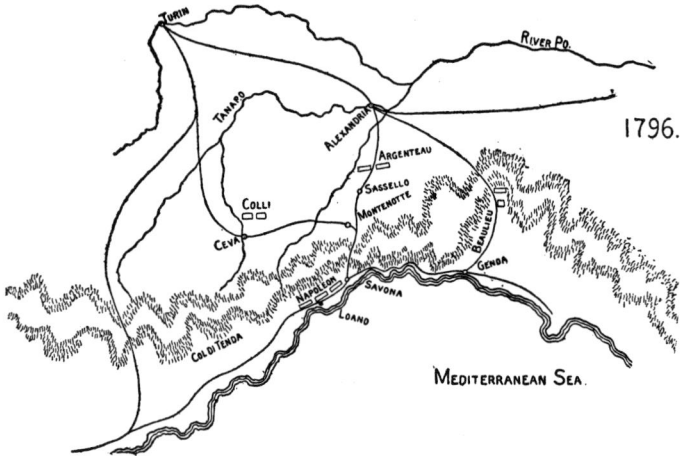

Genoa. His right wing consisted of the Piedmontese
army under Colli at Ceva; his centre was at Sassello; with
his left he was reaching out to join hands with the English
at Genoa. Kellerman faced, in the passes of the Alps, a
force of twenty-five thousand Sardinians, but for the moment was out of the business.

Napoleon spent but few days in providing for his troops,
and then began to concentrate on his right flank at
Savona. He knew that his own position was weak, but
he also divined from the reports brought in from the out-

posts that the enemy's was worse. From the very start he enunciated in his strategic plan the maxim he obeyed through life : Move upon your enemy in one mass on one line so that when brought to battle you shall outnumber him, and from such a direction that you shall compromise him. This is, so to speak, the motto of Napoleon's success. All perfect art is simple, and after much complication or absence of theoretical canons from ancient times to his, Napoleon reduced strategy down to this beautifully simple, rational rule.

Nothing in war seems at first blush so full of risk as to move into the very midst of your enemy's several detachments. No act in truth is so safe, if his total outnumbers yours and if you outnumber each of his detachments. For, as always seemed to be more clear to Napoleon and Frederick than to any of the other great captains, you can first throw yourself upon any one of them, beat him and then turn upon the next. But to do this requires audacity, skill, and, above all, tireless legs. And success is predicated in all cases on the assumption that God is on the side of the heaviest battalions.

So Napoleon, who was very familiar with the topography of Italy, at once determined to strike Beaulieu's centre, and by breaking through it, to separate the twenty-five thousand Piedmontese in the right wing from the thirty-five thousand Austrians in the left wing, so that he might beat each separately with his own thirty-seven thousand men.

Beaulieu's reaching out toward Genoa facilitated Napoleon's manœuvre, for the Austrian would have a range of mountains between him and his centre under Argenteau, whom he had at the same time ordered forward on Savona via Montenotte. Napoleon's manœuvre was strategically a rupture of Beaulieu's centre. Tactically it first led to an attack on the right of Argenteau's column. The details of the manœuvre it would consume hours to follow. Suffice it to say that by a restless activity which, barring Frederick, had not been seen in war since the days of Cæsar, Napoleon struck blow after blow, first upon Argenteau, throwing him back easterly, then on Colli, throwing him back westerly, absolutely cut the allies in two, fought half a dozen battles in scarce a greater number of days, and in a short fortnight had beaten the enemy at all points, had captured fifteen thousand prisoners, fifty guns, and twenty-one flags.

Still the problem was serious. Beaulieu, if active, could shortly concentrate one hundred thousand men. Napoleon must allow him not a moment of breathing spell. He issued a proclamation to his troops which sounds like the blare of a trumpet. It set ablaze the hearts of his men ; it carried dread to his enemies, and Napoleon followed it up by a march straight on Turin. Alarmed and disconcerted, the King of Sardinia sued for peace. Napoleon concluded an armistice with him, and thus saw himself disembarrassed of the enemy's right wing and free to turn on the left under Beaulieu. His columns were at once launched on Alexandria, and by his skilful manœuvres and unparalleled alertness he soon got the better of the Austrians. He had at a stroke made himself the most noted general of Europe. The rest of the campaign was equally brilliant and successful.

Napoleon had shown his army that be commanded not

by the mere commission of the Directory, but by the divine right of genius. He had not only taken advantage of every error of his opponents, but had so acted as to make them commit errors, and those very errors of which he had need. His army had been far from good. But " I believe," says Jomini, " that if Napoleon had commanded the most excellent troops he would not have accomplished more, even as Frederick in the reversed case would not have accomplished less."

We recognize in this first independent campaign of Napoleon the heroic zeal of Alexander, the intellectual subtlety of Hannibal, the reckless self-confidence of Cæsar, the broad method of Gustavus, the heart of oak of Frederick. But one fault is discoverable, and this, at the time, was rather a virtue, — Napoleon underrated his adversary. By and by this error grew in the wrong direction, and became a strong factor in his failures.

Through the rest of this campaign, which numbered the victories of Lodi, Castiglione, Bassano, Arcole, the most noteworthy thing except his own personal diligence is the speed with which Napoleon manœuvred his troops. To state an instance : from September 5 to September 11, six days, Napoleon's men fought one pitched battle and two important combats and marched, Masséna eighty-eight miles, Augereau ninety-six miles, and the other corps less distances. He was far from being uniformly lucky. He had many days of serious backsets. But whenever luck ran in his favor, he seized it and made it useful ; when against him, he gamely strove to stem its tide. If Fortune frowned, he wooed her unceasingly till she smiled again.

The campaign which began in April, 1796, really lasted till April, 1797. Napoleon pushed the Austrians out of Italy and well back towards Vienna. His triumphs culminated in the brilliant victory of Rivoli, and his success at the truce of Leoben. At Rivoli, with thirty thousand men, Napoleon defeated the enemy and captured twenty thousand prisoners. The men who had left Verona and fought at San Michele on the 13th of January, marched all night to Rivoli, there conquered on the 14th, and again marching to Mantua, some thirty miles, compelled Provera to lay down his arms on the 15th. Napoleon could rightfully boast to have equalled Cæsar in speed of foot.

The men of the Revolution had cut loose from eighteenth century methods of warfare by rising *en masse* and putting the personal element into the scale. But it was reserved for Napoleon to substitute a new method for the old. From Nice to Leoben he showed the world what modern war can do. He made himself independent of magazines, as Frederick had done but rarely. With a smaller army he always had more men at the point of contact. This was Napoleon's strongest point. He divined what his enemy would do, not from his tent but from the saddle, seeing with his own eyes and weighing all he saw and heard. He was every day and all day long in motion; he rode unheard-of distances. He relied on no one but himself, as, with his comparatively small army, h could well do; and correctly seeing and therefore correctly gauging circumstances, he had the courage to act upon his facts. He sought battle as the result of every manœuvre. The weight of his intellect and his character were equally thrown into all he did. And his abnormal ambition drove him to abnormal energy. In this his first campaign and in one year, with moderate forces, he had advanced from Nice to within eighty miles of Vienna, and had wrung a peace from astonished Austria.

Napoleon next undertook the Egyptian campaign. His ambition had grown with success. But matters in France were not in a condition of which he could personally avail, and he believed he could increase his reputation and power by conquests in the East. His imagination was boundless. Perhaps no great soldier can be free from imagination, or its complement, enthusiasm. Napoleon had it to excess, and in many respects it helped him in his hazardous undertakings. At this time he dreamed himself another Alexander conquering the Eastern world, thence to return, as Alexander did not, with hordes of soldiers disciplined by himself and fanatically attached to his person, to subjugate all Europe to his will. The narration of this campaign of sixteen months may be made to sound brilliant; its result was miscarriage. It is full of splendid achievements and marred but by one mishap, — the siege of Acre. But the total result of the campaign was failure to France, though gain to Napoleon, who won renown, and, abandoning his army when the campaign closed, returned to Paris at a season more suited to his advancement. Napoleon's military conduct in this campaign shows the same marvellous energy, the same power of adapting means to end, of keeping all his extraordinary measures secret, the better to impose on the enemy by their sudden development, the same power over men. But the discipline of the army was disgraceful. The plundering which always accompanied Napoleon's movements — for, unlike Gustavus and Fred-crick, he believed in allowing the soldier freedom beyond bounds if only he would march and fight — was excessive. The health of the army was bad; its deprivations so great that suicide was common to avoid suffering which was worse. And yet Napoleon, by his unequalled manage-ment, kept this army available as a tool, and an excellent one.

Napoleon now became First Consul. The campaign of 1800 was initiated by the celebrated crossing of the Alps. This feat, of itself, can no more be compared, as it has been, to Hannibal's great achievement, nor in-deed to Alexander's crossing the Paropamisus, than a Pullman excursion to Salt Lake City can be likened to Albert Sidney Johnston's terrible march across the Plains in 1857. Napoleon's crossing was merely an incident deftly woven into a splendid plan of campaign. From Switzerland, a geographical salient held by them, the French could debouch at will into Italy or Germany. Mélas, the Austrian general in Italy, had his eyes fixed upon Masséna in Genoa. A large reserve army was collected by Napoleon in France, while Moreau pushed toward the Danube. Mélas naturally expected that the French would issue from Provence, and kept his outlook

towards that point. When Napoleon actually descended
from the Great St. Bernard upon his rear, he was as
badly startled as compromised. This splendid piece of
strategy was followed up with Napoleon's usual restless
push, and culminated in the battle of Marengo. This

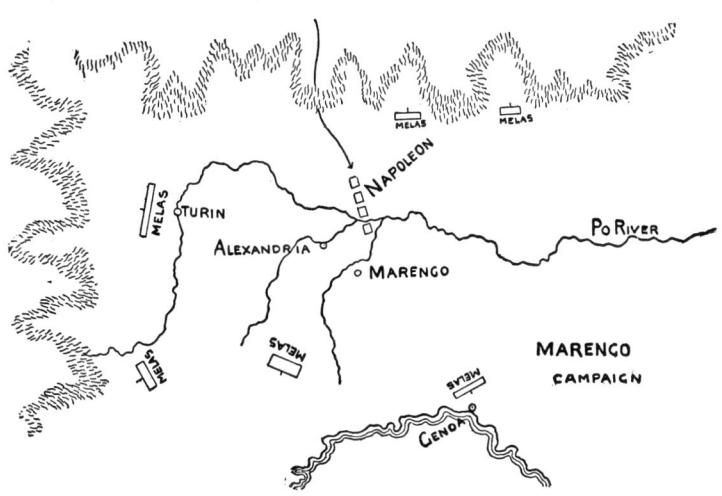

was at first a distinct Austrian victory, but good countenance, Mélas' neglect to pursue his gain, and Napoleon's ability to rally and hold his troops until
absent Dessaix could rejoin him, turned it into an
overwhelming Austrian defeat. And Napoleon, by the
direction given to his mass, had so placed Mélas that
defeat meant ruin. He was glad to accept an armistice
on Napoleon's own terms.

This superb campaign had lasted but a month, and
had been characterized by the utmost dash and clear-

ness of perception. Again Napoleon's one mass projected on one properly chosen line had accomplished wonders.

Napoleon once said to Jomini, "The secret of war lies in the secret of communications. Keep your own and attack your enemy's in such a way that a lost battle may not harm you, a battle won may ruin your adversary. Seize your enemy's communications and then march to battle." Napoleon's success came from study of the situation. His art was founded on an intimate knowledge of all the facts, coupled with such reasoning power as enabled him to gauge correctly what his enemy was apt to do. Without the art the study would be useless. But the art could not exist apart from study.

After Marengo there were five years of peace. These and the four years between Wagram and the Russian campaign were the only two periods of rest from war in Napoleon's career. Succeeding this came the memorable Austerlitz campaign. Napoleon had had for some months three of his best officers in Germany studying up topography, roads, bridges, towns, in the Black Forest region and toward the Tyrol and Bohemia. To thus make himself familiar with the status was his uniform habit.

Napoleon, now Emperor, was at Boulogne, threatening and perhaps at times half purposing an invasion of England. He commanded the best army he ever had. The Austrians, not supposing him ready, inundated Bavaria with troops, without waiting for their allies, the Russians, and marched up the Danube to the Iller,

under Field-Marshal Mack. Napoleon put an embargo
on the mails, broke up from Boulogne at twenty-four
hours' notice, and reached the vicinity of the enemy
with an overwhelming force before Mack was aware of
his having left the sea. His line of march was about

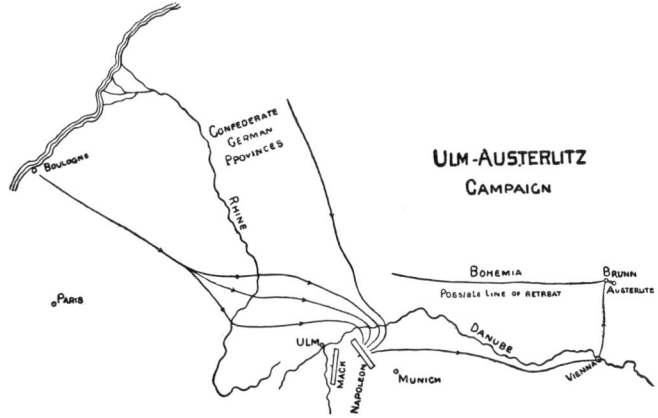

Mack's right flank, because this was the nearest to
Boulogne and gave him a safe base on the confederate
German provinces. So well planned was the manœuvre,
so elastic in its design for change of circumstances, that
it fully succeeded, step for step, until Mack was surrounded at Ulm and surrendered with his thirty thousand
men. Here again we find the Napoleonic rule fairly
overwhelming Mack with superior numbers. Except
in 1796 and 1814, Napoleon always had more men
than the enemy on the field at the proper time. "They
ascribe more talent to me than to others," he observed,

"and yet to give battle to an enemy I am in the habit of beating, I never think I have enough men; I call to my aid all that I can unite."

The chart herewith given of the grand manœuvre of Ulm is so simple as to suggest no difficulties of execution. But there is probably nothing in human experience which taxes strength, intellect, judgment, and character to so great a degree as the strategy and logistics of such a move-ment, unless it be the tactics of the ensuing battle. The difficulties are, in reality, gigantic.

Napoleon headed direct for Vienna, and on the way absolutely lived on the country. " In the movements and wars of invasion conducted by the Emperor, there are no magazines ; it is a matter for the commanding generals of the corps to collect the means of victualling in the coun-tries through which they march," writes Berthier to Mar-mont. Napoleon took Vienna and marched out towards Brünn, where the Austrians and Russians had concentrated. Here he was far from secure, if equal talent had been opposed to him ; but he took up a position near Austerlitz, from which he could retreat through Bohemia, if necessary, and, calmly watching the enemy and allowing several chances of winning an ordinary victory to pass, he waited, with an audacity which almost ran into braggadocio, for the enemy to commit some error from which he could wrest a decisive one. And this the allies did, as Napoleon divined they would do. They tried to turn his right flank and cut him off from Vienna. Napoleon massed his forces on their centre and right, broke these in pieces, and won the victory of which he was always most proud. Napoleon's conduct here showed distinctly a glint of what he himself so aptly calls the divine part of the art.

There is always a corresponding danger in every plan which is of the kind to compass decisive results. In this case Napoleon risked his right wing. But to judge how much it is wise to risk and to guess just how much the enemy is capable of undertaking is a manifestation of genius.

The era of the great battles of modern war dates from Austerlitz. Marengo was rather two combats than one great battle. Frederick's battles were wonders of tactics and courage, but they differ from the Napoleonic system. In Frederick's battles the whole army was set in motion for one manœuvre at one time to be executed under the management of the chief. If the manœuvre was interrupted by unforeseen events, the battle might be lost. In Napoleon's system, the centre might be broken and the wings still achieve victory ; one wing might be crushed while the other destroyed the enemy. A bait was offered the enemy by the exhibition of a weak spot to attract his eye, while Napoleon fell on the key-point with overwhelming odds. But in this system the control passed from the hand of the leader. All he could do was to project a corps in a given direction at a given time. Once set in motion, these could not readily be arrested. Such a system required reserves much more than the old method. "Battles are only won by strengthening the line at a critical moment," says Napoleon. Once in, Napoleon's corps worked out their own salvation. He could but aid them with his reserves.

There is a magnificence of uncertainty and risk, and

corresponding genius in the management of the battles of Napoleon; but for purely artistic tactics they do not appeal to us as do Frederick's. The *motif* of Alexander's battles is more akin to Napoleon's; that of Hannibal's, to Frederick's.

It has been said that Napoleon never considered what he should do in case of failure. The reverse is more exact. Before delivering a battle, Napoleon busied himself little with what he would do in case of success. That was easy to decide. He busied himself markedly with what could be done in case of reverse.

Like all great captains, Napoleon preferred lieutenants who obeyed instead of initiating. He chafed at independent action. This was the chief's prerogative. But as his armies grew in size he gave his marshals charge of detail under general instructions from himself. Dependence on Napoleon gradually sapped the self-reliance of more than one of his lieutenants, and though there are instances of noble ability at a distance from control, most of his marshals were able tacticians, rather than great generals. Napoleon grew impatient of contradiction or explanation; and he sometimes did not learn or was not told of things he ought to know. He was no longer so active. Campaigning was a hardship. His belief in his destiny became so strong that he began to take greater risks. Such a thing as failure did not exist for him. His armies were increasing in size, and railroads and telegraphs at that day did not hasten transportation and news. The difficulties he had to contend with were growing fast.

These things had the effect of making Napoleon's mili-

tary plans more magnificent, more far-reaching. But all
the less could he pay heed to detail, and from now on one
can, with some brilliant exceptions, perceive more errors
of execution. In the general conception he was greater
than ever, and this balanced the scale. His ability to put
all his skill into the work immediately in hand was marvellous. But with a vast whole in view, the parts were,
perhaps of necessity, lost sight of.

The campaigns of 1806 and 1807 were in sequence.
To move on the Prussians, who, under the superannuated
Duke of Brunswick, were concentrated in Thuringia,
Napoleon massed on his own right, disgarnishing his left,
turned their left, — in this case their strategic flank,
because the manœuvre cut them off from Berlin and their
allies, the Russians, — and with overwhelming vigor fell
on the dawdling enemy at Jena and Auerstädt. The
Prussians had remained stationary in the art of war where
they had been left by Fredcrick, and had lost his burning
genius.

It was at the outset of this campaign that Jomini
handed in to Marshal Ney, his chief, a paper showing
what Napoleon must necessarily do if he would beat the
Prussians and cut them off from their approaching allies.
He alone had divined the strategic secrets of the Emperor.

In this campaign we plainly see the growth of risk com-
mensurate within the magnitude of plan, but we also recognize the greater perfection of general intuitions, the larger
plan and method. Details had to be overlooked, but the
whole army was held in the Emperor's hand like a battalion in that of a good field-officer. In forty-eight hours

his two hundred thousand men could be concentrated at any one point. And the very essence of the art of war is to know *when* you may divide, to impose on the enemy, subsist, pursue, deceive, and to know *how* to divide so that you may concentrate before battle can occur.

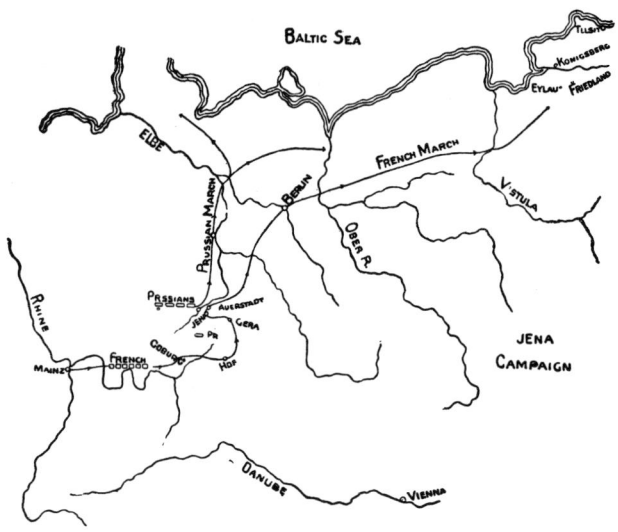

Again Napoleon had carried out his principle of moving on one line in one mass on the enemy, and a few great soldiers began to see that there was a theory in this. Jomini first grasped its full meaning and showed that only battle crowns the work. Without it a general is merely uncovering his own communications. Victory is essential to the success of such a plan. Napoleon pushed restlessly in on the enemy. "While others are in council, the French army is on the march," quoth he.

In the Austerlitz and Jena campaigns, Napoleon's manœuvre was so admirably conceived that he kept open two lines of retreat, which he could adapt to the enemy's evolutions, — at Austerlitz via Vienna and Bohemia, at Jena still more secure lines on the Rhine and on the Main or Danube. This is a distinct mark of the perfection of the plans.

The succeeding Friedland campaign has several items of interest. At his first contact with the Russians, Napoleon, instead of sticking to his uniform plan of one mass on one line, tried to surround his enemy before he knew where the tactical decision of the campaign would come. Result, a thrust in the air by one corps, another did not reach the appointed place, a third met unexpected and superior forces, and the enemy broke through the net. Napoleon seemed to be experimenting. The captain of 1796, Ulm, Jena, is for the moment unrecognizable.

The Russians attacked Napoleon in his winter-quarters, and the bloody and indecisive battle of Eylau resulted, where for the first time Napoleon met that astonishing doggedness of the Russian soldier, on which Frederick had shattered his battalions at Kunersdorf. Later came the victory of Friedland. Napoleon's order for this day is a model for study. Every important instruction for the battle is embraced in the order; details are left to his lieutenants. Only the time of launching the first attack is reserved to the chief. But the strategy of the Friedland campaign was not so crisp. The true manœuvre was to turn the Russian left, their strategic flank, and throw them back on the sea. Napoleon turned their right to cut them off from Königsberg. It was mere good luck that Friedland ended the campaign. Even after defeat the enemy could have escaped.

In the Spanish campaign of the winter of 1807–8, Napoleon reverted to his 1796 manœuvre of breaking the enemy's centre. But Napoleon had undertaken what could not be accomplished, — the subjugation of Spain. His own strategy and the tactics of his marshals were both brilliant and successful ; he could have compelled a peace, had such been the object. But to subdue a people fanatically fighting for their homes, in a mountainous country, is practically impossible by any means short of extermination. It was in the political, not the military, task that Napoleon failed.

While Napoleon was struggling in Spain, Austria deemed the occasion good again to assert herself. This gave Napoleon an opportunity of leaving to his lieutenants a game he already saw he could not win, but in which he had achieved some brilliant openings, and hurry to fields on which he felt a positive superiority. His army and allies were already on the scene.

Berthier was in charge, and to him Napoleon had given full and explicit instructions. But Berthier, though a good chief of staff, had no power to grasp a strategic situation. By not obeying orders, he had, by the time Napoleon arrived, muddled the problem, and instead of concentrating behind the Lech, had got Davout's corps pushed out to Ratisbon, where it was liable to be cut off. Napoleon was in perilous case. But by a beautiful and rapid series of manœuvres, in which he cut the enemy in two, he wrought victory out of threatening defeat. He was justly proud of this. " The greatest military manœuvres that I have ever made, and on which I most flatter myself, took place at Eckmühl, and were immensely superior to those of Marengo or other actions which preceded or followed them." It is the rapidity and suddenness of these manœuvres which distinguished them from 1805. There was a regular plan. Here a constant series of surprises and changes.

In making his plans, Napoleon never began by " What can the enemy do ? " but he first sought to place his army in the best position, and then asked, " What now can the enemy do ? " This gave him the initiative. But his plan was always elastic enough to bend to what the enemy might do. He never made plans colored by the enemy's possibilities. He chose his own plan intelligently, according to the geography, topography, and existing conditions, and made it elastic enough to be equal to the enemy's. " The mind of a general should be like the glass of a telescope in sharpness and clearness, and never conjure up pictures." The elasticity of Napoleon's Eckmühl plan is well shown by his ability to turn threatening disaster into brilliant success.

During all these days, Napoleon was tremendously active. He was personally at the important points. He hardly ate or slept. His body was governed entirely by his will. The soldier of 1796 was again afoot. But he was well and hearty. The lapse he now made is all the more singular. The Archduke Charles had been beaten at Eckmühl and was retiring into Ratisbon to cross the Danube ; Napoleon neglected to pursue. They say he was persuaded by his marshals that the troops were too tired. For the first time in his life he succumbed to an obstacle. " Genius consists in carrying out a plan despite obstacles, and in finding few or no obstacles," he once said.

Failure to pursue may come from the difficulty of leaving one's magazines, as in Frederick's era, or because the captain is exhausted, as well as the troops. But if the captain wants to pursue, the troops can always do so. If the enemy can fly, the victor can follow. Some part of the army is always in condition to march.

Jomini says that if Napoleon had here pursued like the Prussians after Waterloo, it would have greatly modified the campaign. As it was, the Archduke made good his escape. Napoleon had broken in between the two wings of the Austrian army, but he had not crippled the one before turning against the other. So that when he reached Vienna on the heels of the left, he found ready to meet him the right wing, which he ought to have crushed beyond so quick recovery at Ratisbon. This failure to pursue is the first symptom of a habit which from now on is more observable of not utilizing every advantage.

Then followed the crossing of the Danube at Lobau and the battles around Aspern and Essling, which terminated with defeat and great loss. The Archduke was on hand, received in overwhelming numbers that part of the French army which crossed ; the bridges were broken behind the French ; and a disastrous retreat to Lobau followed.

Napoleon's difficulties were growing apace with the size of his armies, and he was now opposed by abler men. But it also seems as if occasional fits of apathy or impatience of exertion were growing on him. His splendid energy at

Eckmühl did not continue. Details received less personal attention. He was more rarely at the front. He began to rely on the eyes of others more than, with his ancient vigor, he would have done— despite his dictum that "a general who sees through the eyes of others will never be in condition to command an army as it should be commanded." Until battle actually opened, he lacked his old enthusiasm. After the first gun he was himself again. But his method of conducting war was no longer so crisp as of yore. He was more daring than careful; he relied on his luck, and strove to cover errors of omission by stupendous blows. He was suffering from not having about him a well-educated, properly selected staff, each member drilled in his specific duties. Till now Napoleon had been his own staff; but with lessening activity, he had no one on whose eyes and judgment he could rely. "The general staff is so organized that one cannot see ahead at all by its means," said he in the next campaign. Still it must constantly be borne in mind that one hundred and fifty thousand men cannot be commanded as readily as forty thousand. And Napoleon's breadth of view, his power of grasping the *tout ensemble*, were still present in greater measure ; and when he chose he could summon up all his old spirit.

Succeeding this defeat were the skilful preparations for a new crossing and battle, the putting over from Lobau of one hundred and fifty thousand men and four hundred guns in one night, and the victory of Wagram. Truly a marvellous performance ! The strength of mind and constancy displayed by Napoleon on Lobau recalls the elastic courage of Alexander when, cut off from his communications, he turned upon the Persians at Issus. But after Wagram the Austrians retired in good order and Napoleon did not pursue. It was no doubt a difficult task, but with the inspiration of his earlier days he would certainly have pushed the Archduke home,—or lost the game. He forgot the principles which had made him what he was, in not following up the retreat. To other and even great generals this criticism could not apply, but Napoleon has created a measure by which himself must be tried and which fits but a limited group. In 1805 he said, "One has but a certain time for war. I shall be good for it but six years more; then even I shall have to stop." Was Napoleon's best term drawing to a close? Or was it that the Archduke Charles was not a Würmser or a Mack?

In Napoleon's battles, tactical details are made to yield to strategic needs. Frederick generally chose his point of attack from a strictly tactical standpoint. Napoleon did not appear to consider that there were such things as tactical difficulties. He always moved on the enemy as seemed to him strategically desirable, and with his great masses he could readily do so. The result of Napoleon's battles was so wonderful, just because he always struck from such a strategic direction as to leave a beaten enemy no kind of loophole. But Napoleon would have been more than human if his extraordinary successes had not finally damaged his character. It is but the story of Alexander with a variation. In the beginning he was, after securing strategic value, strenuous to preserve his tactical values. By and by he began to pay less heed to these ; stupendous successes bred disbelief in failure ; carelessness resulted, then indecision. Those historians who maintain that Napoleon succumbed solely to the gigantic opposition his status in Europe had evoked, can show good reasons for their belief, for Napoleon's task was indeed immense. But was he overtaxed more than Hannibal, Cæsar, or Frederick?

In the Russian campaign (1812) Napoleon's original idea was to turn the Russian right, but finding the Russian position further north than he expected, he resorted to breaking the Russian centre. It here first became a question whether the rule of one mass on one line, distinctly sound with smaller armies, will hold good with the enor- mous armies of 1812 or of modern days ; whether the mere manœuvre may not become so difficult of execution as to open the way to the destruction of the entire plan by a single accident. Certainly its logistics grow to a serious problem with a force beyond two hundred thousand men, and it seems probable that when armies much exceed this figure, the question of feeding, transportation, and command, even with railroads and telegraph, make concentric operations more available. And the fact that even Napoleon could not, in the absence of a thoroughly educated staff and perfectly drilled army, obtain good results from the handling of such enormous forces, gives prominence to the value of the Prussian idea of placing greater reliance on an army drawn from the personal service of the people and made perfect in all its details from the ranks up, than on the genius of a single general.

The entire plan of the Russian campaign was consistent

and good. The Bonaparte of 1796 would probably have carried it through, despite its unprecedented difficulties. But its execution was seriously marred by the absence of Napoleon at the front, and the want of his ancient decisiveness. To be sure he had nearly half a million men to command and feed; but he was no longer the slim, nervously active, omnipresent man. He was corpulent, liked his ease, and shunned bad weather. This want appears in his long stay in Wilna, his failure to put his own individuality into the details of the advance; his now relying on his lieutenants, whom he had never trained, and some of whom were unable, to rely on themselves. Napoleon began to draw his conclusions, not from personal observation, but from assumed premises. He had from the beginning the habit of underrating the enemy's forces. It now grew to be a rule with him to take one-third off from what the enemy really had and double his own forces, in order to encourage his subordinates. This exaggerated reckoning could not but lead to evil. There is none of Frederick's straightforward dependence on his own brain and his army's courage. The king's frankness stands out in high relief against Napoleon's simulation.

But we must constantly bear in mind that Napoleon led an army of unprecedented size, made up of different nationalities, in a limitless territory, and that his difficulties were enormous. It should be noted that Alexander's largest army in the field numbered one hundred and thirty-five thousand men; Hannibal's less than sixty thousand; Cæsar's about eighty thousand; Gustavus' never reached eighty thousand men; Frederick had to parcel out his

forces so that of his one hundred and fifty thousand men
he rarely could personally dispose of more than fifty
thousand in one body. Napoleon carried three hundred
and sixty thousand men into Russia. This is not a final
measure of the task, but it stakes out its size.

Some of Napoleon's Russian manœuvres are fully up to
the old ones. The manner of the attempt to turn the
Russian left at Smolensk and seize their communications
so as to fight them at a disadvantage, is a magnificent exhibition of genius. But at the last moment he failed. The
spirit of his plan was to seize the communications of his
opponent and force him to fight; the *letter* was to seize
Smolensk. When he reached Smolensk, the Russians had
retired to the east of the city. Napoleon apparently overlooked the *spirit* of his plan, and though he could easily
have done so, he did not cut the Russians off by a tactical
turning movement. He was not personally where he
needed to be, — on the right, — but remained at his head-
quarters. It may be claimed that the commander of so
huge an army must necessarily remain at central head-
quarters. It is rather true that his administrative aide
should be there, and he at the point of greatest importance. At Smolensk, theoretically and practically, this
was the right, and operations at this point were intrusted
to by no means the best of his subordinates. Napoleon's
intellect was still as clear as ever. It was his physique
and his power of decision which were weakening. Even
allowing the utmost to all the difficulties of the situation,
if tried by the rule of 1796 or 1805, this seems to be in-
disputable.

When Napoleon did not bring on a battle at Smolensk, the Russian campaign had become a certain failure. For it was there settled that he could not reach Moscow with a force sufficient to hold himself. He had crossed the Niemen with three hundred and sixty-three thousand men. At Moscow he could have no more than one hundred thousand. Arrived at Smolensk he was called on to face retreat, which was failure; or an advance to Moscow, which was but worse failure deferred, — almost sure annihilation. This seems clear enough from the military standpoint. But Napoleon advanced to Moscow relying largely on the hope that the Russians would sue for a peace. For this dubious hope of the statesman, Napoleon committed an undoubted blunder as a captain. It is hard to divorce the statesman from the soldier. All great captains have relied on statecraft, and properly so. But such was the purely military syllogism.

Much has been written about Napoleon's failure to put the guard in at Borodino. Under parallel conditions at an earlier day, he would certainly have done so. That he did not is but one link more in the growing chain of indecisiveness. But had he done so, and won a more complete victory, would it have made any eventual difference? Smolensk was his last point of military safety. Even had he been able to winter in Russia, it is not plain how spring would have bettered his case, in view of the logistic difficulties and of the temper of the Russian emperor and people. Time in this campaign was of the essence.

Once or twice on the terrible retreat, Napoleon's old fire and decision came to the fore, but during the bulk of it he was apparently careless of what was happening. He habitually left to his generals all but the crude direction of the outlying corps. The contrast between Napoleon in this disaster and Napoleon after raising the siege of Acre, or after the defeat at Aspern and Essling, is marked. He did not oppose his old countenance to misfortune.

After this campaign, in which the grand army of half a million men was practically annihilated, Napoleon showed extraordinary energy in raising new troops, and actually put into the field, the succeeding spring, no less than three hundred and fifty thousand men. They were not the old army, but they were so many men. Napoleon understood this : " We must act with caution, not to bring bad troops into danger, and be so foolish as to think that a man is a soldier." He had thirteen hundred guns. " Poor soldiers need much artillery." The lack of good officers was the painful feature. The few old ones who were left were ruined by bad discipline. The new ones were utterly inexperienced.

In the campaign of 1813, Napoleon showed all his old power of conception. The intellectual force of this man never seemed overtaxed. But the lack of resolution became still more marked. He began by winning two battles, — Lützen and Bautzen, — in which he freely exposed himself and worked with all his old energy, to lend his young troops confidence. He was then weak enough to enter into an armistice with the allies. This was a singularly un-Napoleonic thing to do. He had turned the enemy's right and was strategically well placed. It was just the time to push home. If the reasons he alleged —

want of cavalry and fear of the dubious position of
Austria — were really the prevailing ones, Napoleon was
no longer himself, for his wonderful successes hitherto
had come from bold disregard of just such things.

Napoleon here shows us how often fortune is of a man's
own making. So long as he would not allow circumstances to dictate to him, fortune was constant. When he
began to heed adverse facts, we see first indecisive victories, then half successes, and by and by we shall see
failure and destruction.

The operations about and succeeding Dresden show a
vacillation which contrasts with the intellectual vigor.
For the first time Napoleon conducted a defensive campaign. He studied his chances of an offensive, and cast
them aside for reasons which would not have weighed a
moment with him in 1805. And yet the defensive against
his concentrically advancing enemies was no doubt the best
policy. It shows Napoleon's judgment to have been better
than ever. After this brilliant victory Napoleon ordered a
pursuit — which he ought to have made effective — across
the Erzgebirge, but without issuing definite instructions.
Sickness forbade the personal supervision he had expected
to give; troops intended to sustain the advanced corps
were diverted from this duty by a sudden change of purpose. Here was, as Jomini says, "without contradiction,
one of Napoleon's gravest faults." But Napoleon had got
used to seeing things turn in his favor, until he deemed
constant personal effort unnecessary. Decreasing strength
had limited his activity; great exertion was irksome. The
immediate result of this ill-ordered operation was the de·

struction of a corps; the secondary result, the re-encouragement of the allies, whose *morale* had been badly shaken by three defeats, and whose main army he should have followed into Bohemia and broken up. The grand result was loss of time, which to Napoleon was a dead loss, a new advance of the allies, and the battle of Leipsic. During all this time, while Napoleon's execution was weak compared to his old habit, his utterances and orders showed the clearest, broadest conception of what was essential. But he was no longer the man who used to gallop forty to sixty miles a day to use his eyes. Even at Leipsic he exhibited at times his old power; when defeat was certain he lapsed into the same indifference he had shown on the Russian retreat.

Nothing now, in a military sense, could save Napoleon, except to concentrate all his forces into one body and manœuvre against the allies with his old vigor. But the Emperor Napoleon could not bear to give up Italy, Belgium, Spain, as General Bonaparte had given up Mantua to beat the enemy at Castiglione; and he committed the grievous mistake of not concentrating all his forces for the defence of France. The campaign around Paris is a marvel of audacious activity, though indeed it did not bring up any of the larger intellectual problems of Marengo, Ulm, or Jena. If Napoleon had done half as good work with the larger army he might have had, there is scarce a doubt but that he would have gone far towards peace with honor. As it was, he was crushed by numbers. But no words can too highly phrase his military conduct, within its limits, in this brief campaign. There is but one mistake, — the underrating of his enemy, the misinterpretation of manifest facts.

The Waterloo campaign (1815), as already said, bears marked resemblance to that of 1796. The details of Waterloo are so well known that only the reasons will be noted which appear to make Napoleon's first so great a success and his last so great a failure.

At the beginning of June, Napoleon had available for Belgium, where he proposed to strike the allied forces, one hundred and ten thousand foot, and thirteen thousand five hundred horse. In Belgium were Wellington, covering Brussels with ninety-five thousand men, and Blucher lying from Charleroi to Namur with one hundred and twenty-four thousand. Napoleon was superior to either; inferior to both together. He chose against these allied armies the same offensive manœuvre he had employed against Beaulieu and Colli, — a strategic breaking of their centre, so as to separate them and attack each one separately. The controlling reasons were the same. The allies were of different nationalities, and each had a different base, as well as varying interests. If cut in two they no doubt would retire eccentrically, of which Napoleon could take immediate advantage. The key to the whole problem was the exhibition by him of foresight, boldness, and rapid action. The plan could not be better.

He concentrated on Charleroi. From here led two pikes, one to Brussels, which was Wellington's line of advance and retreat, one to Liège, which was Blucher's. Wellington and Blucher were connected by the Namur-Nivelles road, which cut the other pikes at Quatre-Bras

and near Ligny. In order to push in between the allies to
any effect, Napoleon must seize on both these points.

The French army broke up June 15th at 3 A.M.
Napoleon was full of eagerness and early in the saddle.
The French advanced with slight opposition to Quatre-
Bras, and forced the Prussians back to Fleurus. Napoleon

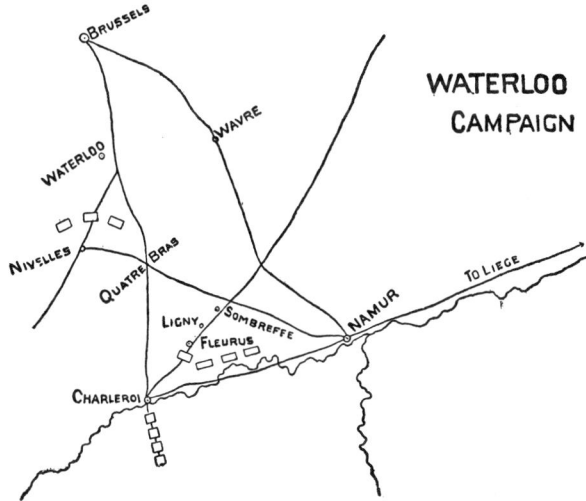

remained in the saddle all day, then retired to Charleroi
overcome with a fatigue which seemed to paralyze his mental faculties. He could no longer conquer sleep as of old.
His bodily condition was bad, and even the necessity of
present success was unable to evoke persistent effort.
There is a singular difference between Napoleon at this
time and grim old Frederick in 1759 suffering from gout.
The king never gave up for an instant his restless work.
Disease and pain could not subdue his obstinate diligence.

The emperor's ailments overcame his zeal. Here began those little lapses of unused time whose addition, in four days, sufficed to bring Napoleon to the end of his career. The plan of campaign was as brilliantly thought out and begun as that of 1796, and with equal vigor would have equally succeeded. Wellington and Blucher had foreseen the manœuvre, and agreed to concentrate for mutual support at Quatre-Bras and Ligny. But Wellington, instead of holding Quatre-Bras, gave Nivelles as the rallying-point. Not even Würmser or Mack could have made an error more in Napoleon's favor, for this separated him from Blucher instead of gaining him his support. Napoleon had the chance to strike Blucher singly. Wellington had not yet assembled. Napoleon should have reached Quatre-Bras and Ligny on the 15th, as he could easily have done, or at a very early hour on the 16th. But no orders even were issued till nearly 9 A.M. of the 16th. In his old days, Napoleon would have been at the outposts at daylight, have gauged the situation with his own eyes and his incomparable power of judgment, and would have attacked at an early hour. But he did not reach the ground till noon nor finish his reconnoissance till 2 P.M. Ney had been sent to Quatre-Bras.

Despite delays, however, part of Napoleon's plan did succeed. Wellington was prevented from joining Blucher, and Blucher was beaten and fell back in disorder. Now Napoleon's object was so to manœuvre as to keep the allies apart. This could be done only by immediate pursuit. He must push on after Blucher relentlessly, so as to throw him off in an easterly direction, where he could observe him with a small force, while he should dispose of Wellington singly. And the more Wellington should manage to push back Ney, the graver danger he would run.

Nothing was done about the pursuit of Blucher on the night of 16th to 17th. Next morning Napoleon leisurely visited the battle-field of Ligny and conversed with his officers about indifferent things. None of the old-time drive was manifest. It was again noon before he ordered Grouchy in pursuit of the Prussians, while he himself would turn against the English. Grouchy got off about 2 P.M. No one knew at that time whether Blucher had retired on Namur or Wavre. In earlier days Napoleon would have ascertained this fact with his own eyes, *for it was the one fact to make no mistake about.* Whether to ascertain this was the duty of the staff or the general is immaterial. That Napoleon did not do so may not have been his fault; but it was his misfortune. Great captains have won success by personal activity and by relying only on themselves in critical matters. In estimating a great soldier, one must number all his errors of omission and commission. No general may shelter himself behind the lapse of a subordinate. He must stand or fall by what he himself does or fails to do.

But the fate of the campaign was already sealed. Blucher had had the night of the 16th to 17th, and the morning of the 17th, and he had used the respite well. He boldly threw up his own base on Liège and marched on Wavre to rejoin Wellington. Napoleon had assumed that Blucher would retire along his line of communications. He desired him to do this, and erroneously calculated on his having done so. The object of breaking the allied centre, the sundering of the allies so as to beat them in detail, had been forfeited by the sixteen or eighteen hours of unnecessary delays after the battle of Ligny. The battle of Waterloo itself has been so fully and ably discussed from this rostrum, and Grouchy's part of the failure so clearly explained, that I will go no further. It seems clear that the battle was lost on the day preceding it. If Blucher did not join Wellington by one means he would by another, when Napoleon gave him so many hours leeway. Nothing but the old activity in following up his initial success could possibly have enabled Napoleon to fight Wellington and Blucher separately, — and if they joined they were sure to beat him. Had he kept right on, he would have beaten Wellington, and Blucher would have retired. His difficulties here were not great. He was successful in his early steps, and failed in later ones. The explanation of the whole matter lies in the fact that Napoleon's physical powers and moral initiative had waned. His intellect was unimpaired, but his character had lost its native quality.

No man should be subject to criticism for inability to do his best work when suffering from disease. It is not intended to criticise in this sense. *La critique est facile; l'art est difficile.* The motto of these lectures is that coexistent intellect, character, and opportunity go to make the great captain. We see Napoleon for twelve years possibly the greatest soldier who ever lived. We then see his successes lessen. It was not from declining intellect. It was partly lesser opportunity, — that is, greater difficulties, — partly loss of activity and decisiveness, — or, in other words, character, — proceeding from weakening physique or decrease of moral strength. There may be room for doubt whether failing health alone, or failing health combined with waning character, caused the indecisiveness. It descends into a question of nomenclature. Of the bald fact there can be no doubt. Napoleon at Waterloo was not as great as Napoleon at Austerlitz.

The secret of Napoleon's power lay in his clear eye for facts, his positive mind. Carlyle says: "The man had a certain, instinctive, ineradicable feeling for reality, and did base himself upon fact so long as he had any basis." Napoleon said of himself that he was most of a slave of all men, obliged to obey a heartless master, the calculation of circumstances and the nature of things. Coupled with this were a reliance on facts, rare capacity for divination, and an immense power of imagination. But finally the latter overran the other qualities. His successes convinced him that he could do anything; he forgot what his success had been grounded on, and he began to neglect facts. "It is not possible" is not French, said he. This is the best of maxims construed one way, — the worst, if misconstrued. Napoleon believed himself able to accomplish all things, until his accuracy of judgment was lost in his refusal to look facts in the face. He ceased to be slave of the nature of things. He deserted belief in facts for belief in his destiny. Finally facts became for him not what they were, but what he wished them to be. He refused credit to what did not suit his theory of how things ought to turn.

Napoleon had what rarely coexists, — an equally clear head on the map and in the field. On the map he was able in both theory and practice. His theories are text-books; his letters are treatises. No higher praise can be spoken than to say that every one of Napoleon's fourteen campaigns was, in a military sense, properly planned.

Napoleon showed the value of masses in strategy as well as tactics. In former times the worth of troops was of greater value than numbers. To-day worth of itself is less essential than it was. Napoleon founded his calculations on the equality of thousands. It is he who collated all that was done by the other great captains, clothed it in a dress fit for our own days, and taught the modern world how to make war in perfect form.

Strategy will always remain the same art. Its uses are to-day varied by railroads, telegraphs, arms of precision. What was not allowable in the Napoleonic era can be undertaken now with safety. But all this has only modified, it has not changed strategy. The tendency of modern armies is toward better organization. Ramrod discipline is giving way to dependence on the individuality of officers and men, and to instruction in doing what at the moment is the most expedient thing. But every great soldier will be great hereafter from the same causes which have made all captains what they were; in conducting war he will be governed by the same intellectual and moral strength which they exhibited, and will do, as they always did, what befits the time, unfettered by rules and maxims, but with a broad comprehension of their true value.

Napoleon is so close to this generation that he sometimes appears to us gigantic beyond all others. He certainly moulded into shape the method in use to-day, which the Prussians have carried forward to its highest development by scrupulous preparation in every department, personal service, and the teaching of individuals to act with intelligent independence. That Napoleon was always intellectually the equal, and, in the first part of his career in the moral forces, the equal of any of the captains, cannot be denied. But we must remember that because Napoleon wrought in our own times we can the better appreciate what he did, while our more meagre knowledge of the others makes it impossible to see as clearly the manner in which, to accomplish their great deeds, they must have patterned their means to the work to be done. "The most important qualities of an army leader," says Jomini, "will always be a great character or constitutional courage, which leads to great determinations; *sang froid* or bodily courage which conquers danger; learning appears in third line, but it will be a strong help."

Napoleon exhibited these qualities in full measure up to 1808, and comes close to being, at his best, the greatest of the captains. He failed to exhibit the moral power in as great measure thereafter. It was not years, for Cæsar and

Frederick were older when they showed these same qualities in the highest degree. That Napoleon lost activity
and decisiveness, and thereby forfeited success, is no
reproach. No man can keep his faculties beyond a certain
period. He lacked that equipoise which enables a man to
stand success. He did not last as the others lasted; and
proved that only so long as a man retains the highest
grade of character can he remain a great captain. At
the same time it is but fair to repeat that the conditions
under which Napoleon worked gradually became more
difficult; that the allies learned from him as the Romans
did from Hannibal, and made fewer mistakes as the years
went on; that he was not always able to retain about him
the most efficient of his marshals; that he commanded
vastly larger armies than the other captains. His task was
larger accordingly.

Napoleon's strategy shows a magnificence in conception,
a boldness in execution, and a completeness and homogen-
eity not shown by any other leader. The other captains
can only stand beside him because they builded so that he
might add; they invented so that he might improve. But
while Napoleon reached a height beyond the others, they
did not show the decrease of genius which he showed.

Too little time is left to draw a satisfactory comparison
between Napoleon and his peers in arms. In Frederick
we recognize a man of higher standard than Napoleon
reached. Not merely because Frederick was, of all the
captains, the only one who, with vastly smaller forces, attacked troops equal to his own and defeated them right
and left, — in other words, because he was the typical tac-

tician, the typical fighter, — but because he was steadfast in victory and defeat alike ; because he was so truly a king to his people as well as a soldier ; because he so truly merged his own self in the good of Prussia. Napoleon flared like a comet. Frederick burned like a planet or a fixed star, — less brilliant, less startling, but ever constant. Frederick at the close of his life was the same great man. Napoleon had burned out his lamp. Frederick never waned. Years or infirmity never changed his force or determination, or limited his energies. Moreover, Frederick, like Hannibal, was greater in disaster than in success. Napoleon succumbed to disaster. Frederick and Hannibal alone held themselves against overwhelming civilized armies. They were stronger, more able, more determined, more to be feared the more misfortune crowded upon them. We instinctively couple Napoleon's genius with his greatest success ; we couple Hannibal's or Frederick's with their direst disasters. Alexander and Gustavus never looked real disaster in the face, as Frederick before Leuthen, or Hannibal after the Metaurus. Nor indeed did Cæsar. But Cæsar opposed wonderful countenance to threatening calamity.

Looking at Napoleon and Gustavus, it is perhaps impossible to compare them. Gustavus was immeasurably above all the others in purity of character, and their equal in force and intellect. To him we owe the revival of intellectual war, lost for seventeen centuries ; and on what he did Frederick and Napoleon builded. Napoleon is nearer akin to Cæsar. Perhaps, take them all in all, as soldiers, statesmen, law-givers, Cæsar and Napoleon are the two greatest men. But they sink below the rest in their motives and aspirations. Neither ever lost sight of self; while Alexander's ambition was not only to conquer the East, but to extend Greek civilization; the motive of Hannibal and Frederick was patriotic, and that of Gustavus love of country and religion. Three of the captains were kings from the start. Their ambition was naturally impersonal. Of the other three, Hannibal alone worked from purely unselfish motives.

Nor can we compare Napoleon with Hannibal. In his successes Napoleon is equally brilliant, more titanic; in his failures he falls so far below the level of this great pattern of patient, never-yielding resistance to adversity as to be lost. To Alexander fighting semi-civilized armies, Napoleon can only be likened in his Egyptian campaigns, and in this he in no sense rises to the height of the Macedonian. Napoleon's genius was most apparent on the familiar fields of Europe.

In intellectual grasp, all six great captains stand side by side. In enthusiastic activity and in all the qualities which compel good fortune, Alexander stands clearly at the head. No one but Frederick has perhaps so brilliant a string of tactical jewels as Hannibal, while in a persistent unswerving struggle of many years to coerce success against the constantly blackening frowns of Fortune, Hannibal stands alone and incomparable. Cæsar was a giant in conception and execution alike, and stands apart n having taught himself in middle life how to wage war, and then waging in it a fashion equalled only by the other five. Gustavus will always rank, not only as the man who rescued intellectual war from oblivion, but as the most splendid character, in nobility of purpose and intelligence of method, which the annals of the world have to show. Frederick is not only the Battle Captain who never blenched at numbers, but truly the Last of the Kings, — king and priest, in the history of mankind. Napoleon carries us to the highest plane of genius and power and success, and then declines. We begin by feeling that here is indeed the greatest of the captains, and we end by recognizing that he has not acted out the part. No doubt, taking him in his many-sidedness, Cæsar is the greatest character in history. It may not unfairly be claimed that Napoleon follows next, especially in that he preserved for Europe many germs of the liberty which was born of the blood of the Revolution. Cæsar was the most useful man of antiquity ; Napoleon comes near to being the most useful man of modern times. But neither Cæsar nor Napoleon appeal to us as do splendid, open-hearted Alexander; patient, intrepid, ever-constant Hannibal; the Christian hero, Gustavus; and daring, obstinate, royal Frederick.